Death
and the
Underworld

Discovering Mythology

**Other titles in Lucent Books
Discovering Mythology Series include:**

Gods and Goddesses
Heroes
Monsters
Quests and Journeys

Death and the Underworld

Discovering Mythology

Michael J. Wyly

Lucent Books, an imprint of The Gale Group
10911 Technology Place, San Diego, California 92127

On Cover: *Charon* by Pedro Roviale

Library of Congress Cataloging-in-Publication Data

Wyly, Michael J., 1970–
    Death and the underworld / by Michael J. Wyly.
        p. cm. — (Discovering mythology)
    Includes bibliographical references and index.
    ISBN 1-56006-881-7 (hardback : alk. paper)
1. Death—Mythology—Juvenile literature. [1. Death—Mythology.] I. Title. II. Series.
    BL325.D35 W95 2002
    291.2'3—dc21

                                                      2001003960

Copyright 2002 by Lucent Books, an imprint of The Gale Group
10911 Technology Place, San Diego, California 92127

Printed in the U.S.A.

Contents

Foreword

Created by ancient cultures, the world's many and varied mythologies are humanity's attempt to make sense of otherwise inexplicable phenomena. Floods, drought, death, creation, evil, even the possession of knowledge—all have been explained in myth. The ancient Greeks, for example, observed the different seasons but did not understand why they changed. As a result, they reasoned that winter, a cold, dark time of year, was the result of a mother in mourning; the three months of winter were the days the goddess Demeter missed her daughter Persephone who had been tricked into spending part of her year in the underworld. Likewise, the people of India experienced recurring droughts, weeks and months during which their crops withered and their families starved. To explain the droughts, the Indians created the story of Vritra, a terrible demon who lived in the clouds and sucked up all the world's moisture. And the Vikings, in their search for an understanding of wisdom and knowledge, created Odin, their culture's most powerful god, who gave the world the gift of poetry and possessed two mythic ravens named Thought and Memory.

The idea of myth, fantastic stories that answer some of humanity's most enduring questions, spans time, distance, and differing cultural ideologies. Humans—whether living in the jungles of South America, along the rocky coasts of northern Europe, or on the islands of Japan—all formulated stories in an attempt to understand their world. And although their worlds differed greatly, they sometimes found similar ways of explaining the unknown or unexplainable events of their lives. Other times, there were differences, but the method of explanation—the myth—remains the same.

Each book in the Discovering Mythology series revolves around a specific topic—for example, death and the underworld; monsters; or heroes—and each chapter examines a selection of myths related to that topic. This allows young readers to note both the similarities and differences across cultures and time. Almost all cultures have myths to explain creation and death, for instance, but the actual stories sometimes vary widely. The Babylonians believed that the earth was the offspring of primordial parents, while the Navajo Indians of North America assert that the world emerged over time much like an infant grows into an adult. In ancient Greek mythology, a deceased person passed quickly into the underworld, a physical place that offered neither reward nor punishment for one's deeds in life. Egyptian myths, on the other hand, contended that a person's quality of existence in the afterlife, an ambiguous state of being, depended on his actions on earth.

In other cases, the symbolic creature or hero and what it represents are the same, but the purpose of the story may be different. Although monster myths in different cultures may not always explain the same phenomenon or offer insight into the same ethical quandary, monsters nearly always represent evil. The shape-shifting beast-men of ancient Africa represented the evils of trickery and wile. These vicious animal-like creatures transformed themselves into attractive, charming humans to entrap unsuspecting locals. Persia's White Demon devoured townspeople and nobles alike; it took the intelligence and strength of an extraordinary prince to defeat the monster and save the countryside. Even the Greek Furies, although committing their evil acts in the name of justice, were ugly, violent creatures who murdered people guilty of killing others. Only the goddess Athena could tame them.

The Discovering Mythology series presents the myths of many cultures in a format accessible to young readers. Fully documented secondary source quotes and numerous mythological tales enliven the text. Sidebars highlight interesting stories, creatures, and traditions. Annotated bibliographies offer ideas for further research. Each book in this engaging series provides students with a wealth of information as well as launching points for further discussion.

The Meaning of Death

Perhaps one of the most frustrating elements of life is that an end, death, awaits everyone. It is therefore not surprising that nearly every culture in the world crafted sets of narratives that include detailed rationales for why humans die and what occurs when they do. Within these narratives, called mythologies, one central belief was nearly always present: After death, the soul, ghost, or other invisible remnant of the deceased traveled to an underworld or otherworld reserved for spirits of those who had died.

Humans' belief in the underworld meant that most mythologies supported the idea that some sort of spirit existed within the human body. Thus when death occurred there would be something left of the person that could transcend physical boundaries and enter the spirit world. But even though many peoples envisioned some form of spirit, soul, or ghost, the supposed appearance of the dead in the underworld often differed greatly from culture to culture. The ancient Egyptians thought that the spirit traveled with its body into the world of the dead. In other cultures people believed that the spirit separated itself from the corpse. The traditions of many Native American tribes attribute multiple souls to single individuals.

Since belief in the existence of spirits was universal, the question of where the spirits of the deceased went became central. Thus each mythology typically includes a tangible vision of an afterlife, an eternal resting place of the dead. Yet, just as there were a variety of interpretations of the "spirit" or "soul," concepts of the final resting place also differed markedly.

For some cultures, such as the Greek and African traditions, the land of the dead was located underground, an explanation that was probably a logical extension of burial practices involving underground graves. Other cultures developed stories involving different locations. Some Native American tribes envisioned the land of the dead as located on the earth and therefore accessible to travelers; other tribes placed the land of the dead in the sky or on the tops of unclimbable mountains. The Irish Celts often pictured the land of the dead as a series of faraway islands. Indeed, the location of the inhabitants of the spirit world is often one of the most unique aspects of any particular mythology.

The appearance and function of the land of the dead also varied from culture to culture because of differences in how each one imagined the fate of the deceased upon arrival in the afterlife. Sometimes all deceased persons were believed to share the same fate, meaning that all the dead lived together, en masse, in the same residence. Other traditions taught of an afterlife having different conditions for different people, depending on whether the deceased had lived a moral or immoral life. In cultures that believed poor behavior in life meant that a price must be paid forever in the afterlife, the spirit of the deceased had to be judged by a god or other supernatural force to determine that price. In such a belief system, good behavior always triumphed in the end. As scholar Alan E. Bernstein explains in *The Formation of Hell:*

> What happens to the wicked who die at the height of their wealth and power? Do they ever receive their just deserts? Do they get away with murder? Asserting a measure of justice for those who

Many ancient cultures believed in a land of the dead. An artist depicts the Greek underworld here.

appear to escape into death, suffering no consequences for an evil life, involves many assumptions about providence and postmortem retribution (punishment after death), implying an order on the universe which corrects the apparent excess of evil.[1]

Because various beliefs are possible, fates for the dead vary considerably. Mythologies that do not dictate any specific punishment for the sins of the deceased include those of tribal Africa, in which the dead typically pass without judgment into an underground realm under the leadership of a death god. On the other hand, the death gods of the ancient Egyptians were believed to weigh the hearts of the dead to determine whether they were worthy of eternal life; punishment for the wicked in the Egypt of the pharaohs was nonexistence. And the Aztecs believed that, even though the underworld did not harbor punishment, those who died in battle or submitted to a sacrificial death were rewarded with a special position in the sky with the sun god.

As a result, the afterlife is called by many different names, each reflecting the purpose and function of the land of the dead in a specific culture. Thus when the land of the dead was believed to be underground, the afterlife was often said to take place in the underworld. On the other hand, if the dead were thought to reside in another land on the earth or in the sky, cultures used names such as otherworld and spirit world. Although each term basically refers to the land of the dead, the word chosen in a given case depends on the function and location of the specific culture's death realm.

In addition, some of the myths contain different and even conflicting versions of the underworld's function and location. The details of the Celtic underworld, for example, can vary widely. Some ancient

In this scene from The Egyptian Book of the Dead, *Egyptians watch the balancing of the scales to see if their hearts are pure enough to enter the world of the dead.*

texts, including many of the collected tales of ancient Ireland, might refer to the underworld as a place from which the deceased could never return. Other tales, such as the Welsh story of King Arthur, claim that living heroes can journey to the otherworld temporarily, only to return to the realm of the living at a later date. Regardless of these differences, the role of the land of the dead in all world mythologies is essentially the same: When the dead pass from the world of the living, the spirits move on to another place, illustrating a universal belief in some form of life after death. Similarly, the world of the dead can be seen as an affirmation of life, since in most cultures some have always believed that at least a fragment of each person's humanity has the possibility of living for eternity.

Ancient Egypt: Truth and Judgment

Chapter One

What scholars know of the mythology of the ancient Egyptians is based on the study of graves and tombs, including the pyramids, and scant remaining writings. With the aid of these resources, specialists called Egyptologists have been able to surmise roughly the beliefs associated with the Egyptian underworld and the process by which a dead person might enter it. Fundamental to the understanding of the Egyptian afterlife is the Egyptian concept of *maat*, meaning "truth."

While *maat* is generally translated as "truth," for the ancient Egyptians it was a more complex concept. *Maat* was the truth of the natural world, which means that its definition encompassed the everyday cycles of the sun and moon, the seasonal flooding of the river Nile, and the passing of humankind from life to death. *Maat* also indicated the moral principles by which the Egyptians were expected to abide; for example, stealing or even desiring the possessions of a neighbor was viewed as a transgression against *maat*. As Siegfried Morenz explains in *Egyptian Religion*:

> Maat is right order in nature and society, as established by the act of creation, and hence means, according to the context, what is right, what is correct, law, order, justice and truth. This state of righteousness needs to be pre-

served or established, in great matters as in small. Maat is therefore not only right order but also the object of human activity. Maat is both the task which man sets himself and also, as righteousness, the promise and reward which await him on fulfilling it.[2]

Thus, maat represented both the order of the world and the things a righteous Egyptian had to do within that world to gain access to the afterlife.

Since the dead were thought to be judged based on how well they had lived their lives in accordance with the rules of maat, a living Egyptian who wanted to be rewarded in the afterlife would try to live in accordance with the principles of maat. The idea of maat, therefore, gave the underworld an intimate role in forming the people's perceptions of the world.

Maat and the Natural World

Maat also governed everyday occurrences within the natural world, and even this relationship directly involved the underworld. One of the most powerful and esteemed of the Egyptian gods was the sun god, Ra. The Egyptians believed that Ra

An Egyptian pyramid. Scholars study such structures to learn about the ancient Egyptians' beliefs about death.

The Egyptians believed the sun god Ra (center) died every evening as he passed into the underworld for the night and was then reborn at dawn.

was responsible for making and preserving all things on earth. As is related in the ancient Egyptian text, *The Hymn to the Sun from el-Amarna:*

> Beautiful is your [Ra's] appearing in the horizon of heaven, you living sun, the first who lived! . . . Your rays suckle every field, and, when you arise, they live and thrive for you. You make the seasons in order to sustain all that you have created, the winter to cool them, and the heat (that they may taste you).[3]

Despite the apparent power of the sun god, his life, and therefore the cycles of nature, were intimately linked to the domain of Osiris, ruler of the underworld. The ancient Egyptians believed that Ra died every evening, crossing into the underworld for the length of the night being reborn each morning with the dawn. The cycles of the day and the changing seasons were understood as reflecting, and ordained by, the cyclical existence of Ra himself. Therefore, the underworld, through its intimate association with the *maat*, or cyclical truth, of the natural world, was never far from the thoughts of the living.

14

The Death of Osiris

The history of Osiris begins before he was the ruler of the underworld. The Egyptians believed that, as a mortal, Osiris had ruled over their land during the time before written records were kept. Osiris was seen as a wise and beneficent king who distinguished himself as a religious teacher, a just law-maker, and an instructor, teaching mankind the arts of agriculture. In all these matters, Osiris was aided by his wife, Queen Isis. Thus both monarchs earned the respect and admiration of the majority of their subjects.

But while most people of Egypt appreciated Osiris and Isis, not everyone was content with the royal pair. Set, the brother of Osiris, desired the kingship of Egypt for himself. Thus, he plotted the death of Osiris to make way for his own rise to the throne. To carry out his brother's murder, Set secretly developed alliances with seventy-two conspirators, all members of Osiris's court. In preparation, Set acquired the exact physical measurements of his brother. He then ordered a beautifully decorated wooden chest having the same dimensions as Osiris. When the chest was designed and built, Set brought it into the room where Osiris was dining with many others of his court, including the conspirators.

In the middle of the banquet, Set declared that he would give the beautifully wrought chest to the person whose body could fit perfectly inside it. After

An Egyptian wall painting depicts Osiris, ruler of the underworld.

The Mummy

For the ancient Egyptians, dead mortal's ability to achieve eternal life in the land of the dead depended on the embalming process, which was integral to mummification. The Egyptians believed that to live in the afterlife, one had to mimic the death of Osiris. Therefore, because Isis had embalmed the pieces of Osiris's body, Egyptians believed the bodies of the deceased Egyptians had to be likewise embalmed.

The process of embalming consisted of the removal of the body's inner organs, or viscera, a process called evisceration. The body was then soaked in a solution of natron (a mixture of carbonate and bicarbonate sodas) for many days, and finally every part of the corpse was wrapped in linen bandages. The viscera, namely the liver, lungs, stomach, and intestines, were placed in four different jars, called canopic jars, and each one was dedicated to one of the four sons of Horus. The completed mummy was then provided with a mask that pictured the face of the deceased as it had been in life. Last, the mummy was enclosed in a series of often richly decorated coffins and laid in a burial chamber inside a large tomb known as the House of Eternity.

Egyptian mummies. The ancient Egyptians believed mummification was essential to live in the afterlife.

some debate, cajoling, and teasing, the unsuspecting Osiris was persuaded to lie down inside the chest. As soon as the king was inside, Set and his coconspirators fastened the chest securely, first with nails and then again with melted lead. Set ordered his followers to cast the chest into the Nile River. Deprived of air, food, and water, Osiris died in the tomb that had been made for him.

The current of the river eventually carried the chest bearing the body of Osiris to the Mediterranean Sea. After some time, the chest washed up on the shores of the Byblos region of the Phoenician coast (modern Lebanon). There, a gigantic tree grew around the chest, doubly encasing and protecting the king's corpse.

Devoted Isis

Although the murderous Set was able to take the throne of Egypt, he had not counted on the extraordinary lengths to which Isis, the widowed queen, would be willing to go to restore life to Osiris. On learning of the murder, Isis wandered throughout Egypt and its surrounding lands hoping to find and retrieve her husband's body. She eventually discovered the chest in the course of a visit to the king of the Phoenicians. The king had so admired the tree containing the mysterious chest that he had had it made into a pillar for his palace.

When Isis explained that the tree actually contained her husband's remains, the king relinquished it into her possession. Isis was therefore able to extract the mirac-

ulously preserved body of Osiris and return to Egypt. But the former queen's initial triumph was short-lived. While out hunting, Set accidentally stumbled across the hiding place of the royal corpse. Enraged to find the remains of his brother still intact, Set proceeded to chop the body into fourteen pieces. Afterward, he scattered the pieces throughout the country.

Isis (pictured), the wife of Osiris, was the goddess of fertility.

Once again, Isis traveled throughout Egypt, this time in an effort to locate all the pieces. On finding each piece, Isis prepared it for burial by treating it with preservatives. When she had collected and embalmed all of the pieces, she reassembled the body, which she wrapped in linen, thereby making the first Egyptian mummy. Finally, with the aid of her sister, Nephthys, Isis secretly buried the results of her labor. Afterward, the two women attempted to restore life to the dead king by saying prayers and performing rituals.

Their efforts were partially successful. Osiris was revived, but he was unable to remain in the realm of the living because despite his resurrection, he had already crossed into the Egyptian underworld from which no mortal can depart. Thus Osiris had to relinquish his earthly kingship, but he began to reign the underworld, becoming the death god of the ancient Egyptians. As Bernstein relates: "Having conquered death through his resurrection, Osiris . . . had a claim to jurisdiction [control over], if not outright sovereignty [total power], in the underworld."[4] Thus Osiris was in a position to continue to wield power over the living because, as king of the underworld, he presided over the process by which humans were judged and deemed worthy of eternal life.

The Halls of Osiris

One way that Osiris influenced the living was through his role in the process by which the deceased entered the under-

world; upon their deaths, mortals were judged either to be deserving or undeserving of eternal life. The ancient Egyptians expected this process, believing that their eternal fate would be determined by the good or evil they committed while still alive. Because Osiris was the ruler of the underworld, he presided over the ceremony that determined who had the right to reside in the afterlife with him. Only the deceased found to be deserving were allowed to continue to exist in the underworld; those who were deemed unworthy were destroyed. And this decision was wholly based on whether or not the deceased had lived his life in accordance to the principles of *maat*.

The ancient Egyptians believed that the dead were brought to the great hall of Osiris, called the Hall of Two Truths, to learn of their impending fate. At one end of the hall, the deceased found a shrine resembling a gigantic wooden coffin with a vaulted lid. The ceiling of the shrine was decorated with clusters of grapes, and elaborately carved columns with floral designs supported the vaulted opening. Along the sides of the shrine were forty-two thrones, one for each of the gods of the forty-two districts of Egypt. The gods awaited the approach of the deceased in silence.

At the very rear of the shrine, on his own throne sat Osiris himself. As Alan Shorter describes in *The Egyptian Gods*:

[Osiris is] swathed in white funeral wrappings, or in a tight-fitting costume covered with a design imitat-

This scene from The Egyptian Book of the Dead *shows Egyptians standing before Osiris and proclaiming their worthiness for entrance to the underworld.*

ing a bird's feathers, from which his hands project holding the crook and the whip—scepters of kingship—and the *uas*, a scepter carried only by the gods. His face and hands are . . . colored green, for he represents the vegetation of the earth, continually decaying and reviving, and on his head is . . . set the *atef*-crown. This crown consists of the tall white cap which was used as the crown of Upper Egypt [the northern part of the Nile River delta], with a feather, symbolic of Truth [*maat*], attached to either side, and sometimes ram's horns added below. [5]

As time passed, Osiris was joined by his wife and family. Thus, standing behind Osiris, with their arms embracing his shoulders, were the goddesses Isis and Nephthys, her sister, and in front of him was a lotus blossom upon which were the four sons of Osiris and Isis; the sons presided over the entrails of the deceased which were thought to be necessary for the continuance of life within the underworld.

The Fate of the Enemies of Osiris

A description of the Egyptian underworld in an ancient text titled the *Book of Gates* speaks of the punishment of the enemies of Osiris. Although the exact crimes of these enemies are not clear, it is evident that each managed to offend the death god greatly. Consequently, each of the offenders must submit to horrible tortures. The arms and legs of the enemies are bound together in agonizing positions as the bearded figure of Horus, the son of Osiris, leans forward on his staff and informs the captives of their impending fate. As scholar Alan Shorter describes in *The Egyptian Gods,* Horus says:

Ye shall be hacked to pieces, and shall not exist! Your soul shall be destroyed, it shall not live, because of that which ye did to my father Osiris! . . . O my serpent Khety . . . open thy mouth, unclose thy jaws, belch forth thy fire against the enemies of my father, burn thou up their bodies, consume their souls by this scorching breath of thy mouth, and by the fire that is in thy belly!

Also present were Osiris's assistants, the gods Anubis and Thoth.

Judging the Dead

Upon arrival in Tuat, the land of the dead, the deceased was expected to approach the throne of Osiris and proclaim his or her worthiness by denying having committed forty-two specific sins, one for each of the districts and therefore gods of Egypt. The sins were directly connected to the concept of *maat* since to commit any one of them constituted a violation of the rules of *maat. The Egyptian Book of the Dead* contains the prayers the deceased had to recite to accomplish this. One of the prayers reads,

> O thou being, broad of stride, who
>   comest forth from Heliopolis

[one of the forty-two cities],
I have done no evil!
O thou embracer of flame, who
  comest forth from Kher-aha,
I have not robbed!
O thou Nose, who comest forth
  from Hermopolis,
I have not been covetous
  [desirous]![6]

The deceased recited these prayers until all the standards of conduct imposed by the concept of *maat* had been cited and affirmed.

As the deceased made each declaration, the gods Anubis, who is depicted as having the head of a jackal, and Thoth, traditionally represented with the head of an ibis (a bird that wades in the Nile), carried out a test designed to ascertain the truthfulness of the claims made by the deceased. Since the ancient Egyptians believed that the heart of a sinless person would weigh no more than a feather, they imagined a test in which the heart of the deceased was placed on one side of a balance, and a feather on the other. Alan Shorter elaborates:

> A great balance [scale] stands in the center of the hall . . . and Anubis, jackal-headed, kneels beside it, steadying the swinging pointer with one hand and the right-hand pan [of the scale] with the other. The heart of the dead . . . is placed in one pan, and a feather, symbol of Maat or "Truth," in the other. The human heart was regarded by the Egyptians as the seat of consciousness; hence, if weighed against Truth,

The god Anubis is pictured in an ancient Egyptian fresco. Anubis weighed a dead person's heart against a feather to test the heart's purity.

the accuracy of [the deceased's] protestations of innocence could be tested. As each denial came from his lips he would be judged by his own heart in the balance. If it weighed equal to Truth, then all was well; but if it sank in the scales, then it was heavy with sin and the dead man would stand convicted by the evidence of his own conscience.[7]

It was believed that during this forty-two step process, the deceased attempted to prevent his heart from betraying him. To this end, he was thought to recite the following spell, as found in *The Egyptian Book of the Dead:*

> O my heart of my mother! O my heart of my mother! O my heart of my transformations! Do not stand up against me as a witness! Do not create opposition to me in the council! Do not cause the pan to sink in the presence of the keeper of the balance! Thou art my double which is my body.[8]

Meanwhile Thoth, who was to report the results to Osiris, recorded each movement of the balance. Behind Thoth and Anubis stood the goddess Ammut, also known as the "devourer of the dead" because Ammut consumed the souls of the deceased whose hearts weighed more than the feather. The *Papyrus of Hunefer,* an ancient Egyptian document, describes

this deity's fearsome appearance saying her "forepart is that of crocodiles, her hindquarters those of a hippopotamus, and her middle that of a lion."[9]

Should the heart be heavier than the feather, this fact was dutifully recorded by Thoth, and the dead person was condemned to nonexistence, meaning that his or her soul was utterly destroyed, never to attain eternal life. In these cases, the soul of the deceased was devoured in a single gulp by Ammut so that the person would no longer exist in the mortal world or in the afterlife. For the soul of one who had led a good life, Thoth announced the results of the weighing of the heart to all of the gods in the Hall of Two Truths. According to the *Papyrus of Any,* he said:

> Here ye these words in very truth. I have judged [weighed] the heart. . . . His [the deceased's] character has been proved righteous upon the great balance, and he has been found without crime. He has not diminished the offering-loaves in the temples [he has not stolen from the gods]. He has not falsely reduced the tax-corn [he has not stolen from the government]. He has spoken no idle words [has not participated in malicious gossip] while he was upon the earth.[10]

After Thoth reported the favorable verdict, there remained only the bestowal of the reward: admittance into the kingdom of Osiris, the land of the dead. A dead person so favored would be guided by Horus, son of Osiris and Isis, to the throne of the death god himself. With a nod of his head, Osiris allowed the successful applicant eternal life within the Egyptian underworld. Within the underworld, the deceased resided with all of the other dead who had passed the test in the Hall of Two Truths.

Thoth (pictured) reported the results of the weighing of a deceased's heart to Osiris.

The Sun God and the Underworld

Within Egyptian mythology, the underworld played another role that directly affected the people who continued to exist in the realm of the living, for the land of Osiris was not only the eternal resting place for deceased mortals. It was also the place where the solar disk of the sun, carried by the sun god Ra, disappeared each night in the unending reenactment of the cycle of birth, life, and death. To reflect his descent into the underworld and his ascent into eternal life, Ra assumed many shapes as he journeyed along his arcing path in the daytime sky and as he descended into the dark underworld. With each new form, the sun god also took a new name.

The ancient Egyptians believed that at dawn Ra took the form of a scarab beetle, a sacred shape symbolizing rebirth. In this form, the sun god took the name of Re Khepri, meaning "to become" or "to exist," and he pushed the ball of the sun across the morning sky. With the approach of noon, Re Khepri changed into his most powerful form, that of Ra, a god in human form but with the head of a falcon surmounted by a solar disk (the sun) and a cobra. With the approach of evening, Ra's powerful form deteriorated into that of an old man, called Re Atum, who tottered into the west. With the close of the day, Re Atum entered Tuat, the realm of the dead.

Once in the underworld, the sun god took on a different form altogether. As Shorter explains,

According to the *Book of Him Who Is in the Underworld* [an ancient manuscript], which is generally referred to by scholars under its Egyptian name *Am-Tuat*, the underworld was divided into twelve regions corresponding with the twelve hours of the night, and the Sun-god passed through each region at the appropriate hour. But he himself is very different from the sun of day. His nature has undergone a change, and he is no longer the living Ra but Auf, which means *flesh*, that is to say he is a corpse. Further, he is represented with the head of a ram . . . which was regarded as the soul of Osiris, and the barque [boat] in which he travels sometimes takes the form of a serpent with a head at each end.[11]

Unlike his solo journey across the daytime sky, Ra (now Auf) traveled through the underworld in the company of other immortals who aided him in the nighttime trek, the gods Hu ("Authoritative Utterance"), Saa ("Intelligence"), and Upuaut ("Opener of Roads"). These gods were believed to escort Ra's boat through the twelve regions of the underworld.

Although it is difficult to describe all the sun god's adventures because few works of ancient Egyptian literature survive, some examples do exist. These surviving texts show that in the Sixth Division of the underworld, Ra encountered numerous

The Egyptian Book of the Dead

The Egyptian Book of the Dead *is a term modern Egyptologists use to reference an ancient Egyptian religious text. Following several excavations, archaeologists reconstructed the text from information found written on sheets of papyrus and inscribed on the walls of Egyptian tombs. The Book of the Dead is primarily composed of two early collections of religious literature, the "pyramid texts" and the "coffin texts." The pyramid texts are the prayers and spells found on the interior of burial chambers within the pyramids. These illustrate the early belief that only the rulers of ancient Egypt were allowed to cross over into the afterlife.*

Around 2000 B.C., however, the central government of Egypt collapsed, and the elaborate funerary practices, once reserved for the rulers alone, were appropriated by the common people. This led to the creation of the coffin texts which, while including information from the pyramid texts, also expand on the belief that any person should be able to understand the process by which the dead enter into the underworld, including any prayers and chants the deceased might be expected to intone.

In this scene from *The Egyptian Book of the Dead*, an Egyptian makes an offering to the god Horus (right).

monsters and gods. One example was the serpent, Am-akhu; Shorter says that the Sixth Division was guarded by a "huge serpent, called Am-akhu, *Devourer-of-Spirits*, from whose back four bearded human heads project."[12]

With the arrival of morning, it was said Ra discarded the mummified form of Auf and was transformed into a scarab beetle. Then, Shu, the god of the atmosphere, lifted Ra and the solar disk into the sky, and Ra once again commenced his daily voyage across the heavens.

Thus, newly born from the underworld, dawn arrived to the world of the living in accordance to the *maat*, or truth, that governed nature and its gods. Likewise, the principles of *maat* were believed to govern the fate of humankind, both in the world of the living and in the afterlife of the underworld. Egyptian beliefs in life were therefore connected to the principles by which people were judged upon their deaths. For the ancient Egyptian, the idea of *maat* bound the world of the living to the world of the dead.

Ancient Greece: Mortal Death and Immortal Imprisonment

Unlike the ancient Egyptians who believed that a soul that had not been judged could not enter the afterlife, the ancient Greeks believed that all mortal souls descended to the same place regardless of people's deeds during life. Thus, whether mortals behaved morally or immorally during life, after death, each soul traveled to the land of the death god Hades, a neutral abode that doled out neither punishments nor rewards. Judgment did exist, though, for the Greeks believed that the soul would punish or reward itself by retaining the memory of its life on earth.

For immortals who committed crimes against other gods, the land of the dead functioned strictly as a place of imprisonment. Connected to the underworld was a region located deep underground called

Zeus, ruler of the Greek gods, punished his enemies by banishing them to the darkest corner of the underworld.

influence of Hades over his queen, the goddess Persephone. Thus, the Greek underworld was essentially three worlds in one: home to the souls of humankind, prison for immortals who offended Zeus, and the cause of winter.

The Concept of *Menos*

The fate of humankind in the afterlife was defined by the ancient Greek concept of *menos*, meaning "strength." The belief in *menos* explains how the souls of the dead might suffer in the afterlife even though the god of the dead, Hades, did not punish them directly. The Greeks believed that all souls lacked *menos* and therefore existed only as dream-like reflections of their former selves. The absence of *menos* also caused people to cling to life in their last moments before death; lack of strength also prevented the deceased from moving on from the circumstances of their former lives. Therefore, if the last memories of the deceased were positive, the soul was thought to possess a sense of peace, whereas it was feared that the soul of someone who died in a tormented state of mind would continue to suffer.

Tartarus. Here, the immortal enemies of Zeus, ruler of the gods, were locked away as punishment for their treason.

Lastly, the existence of the underworld also affected the weather. The earth was thought to die each winter because of the

The deceased's trip to the underworld was often depicted as a "journey," yet the exact details of the voyage differ depending on which sources scholars consult. Certain generalizations can be made, though, with respect to the three stages of the journey most commonly cited by experts on ancient Greece.

Each stage is associated with one of three different immortals. The first was Hermes, the messenger of Zeus who wore winged sandals and escorted the deceased to the border of the underworld called Hades like its ruler. Then, on the boat of the immortal Charon, god of the passage to the land of the dead, the deceased crossed the dark River Styx. On the opposite bank, the soul passed through the gates of Hades, which were guarded by Cerberus—a monster that welcomed all dead souls who arrived at the underworld kingdom but attacked those who tried to leave.

Once past the gates of Cerberus, the soul descended through dark passages, carved into the earth, and then finally arrived in the underworld. Even the

Charon navigates the River Styx. A voyage in Charon's boat was one stage in a deceased's journey to the underworld.

Sisyphus, Tantalos, and Ixion

Although the ancient Greeks believed that the dead in Hades were not tortured or punished by the gods, there were exceptions, and eternal torment was the fate of mortals who disrespected the rule of the gods. Indeed, the stories of the crimes and subsequent punishments were meant as lessons to the living who might be tempted to make themselves the equals of the gods.

The first exception was Sisyphus, who revealed a secret affair of Zeus. Sisyphus, who had been king of Corinth, was condemned to roll a rock up a hill only to watch it roll back down again just as he neared the top. This frustrating labor, which Sisyphus was doomed to perform eternally, meant to remind humankind that the secrets of the gods were not for mortals to divulge.

Second was another king, Tantalus, a son of Zeus and a mortal woman, who

Ixion forever spins on a giant wheel in the underworld, his punishment for trying to seduce Zeus's wife.

tried to achieve immortality by stealing it from the gods. His punishment was to remain forever in a lake with fruit trees on its bank. When he tries to drink the water, it dries up, and when he tries to eat the fruit, the wind raises the branches out of reach. This everlasting torture demonstrated that immortality belonged to the gods and would forever lie beyond any mortal's grasp.

The last example was Ixion who tried to seduce the wife of Zeus. For that indiscretion, he was fastened to a wheel, which forever whirled through the air, propelled by underground winds. Ixion's punishment was meant to teach mortals not to try to compete with the gods.

ancient Greeks themselves had difficulty describing Hades. According to one author,

> It seems clear that the Greeks were not much concerned to produce a consistent and clearly mapped-out picture of the landscape of Hades. Nor did they expend much creative energy upon its topography. That the region was regarded as dark and windy, and that it contained a great river, we need not doubt . . . but since we learn of the existence of these attributes from such a variety of literary sources, and since no poet or painter has provided us with a synthesized view, it is perhaps safer to assume that the Greeks were as much in the dark about Hades as they have left us.[13]

However, scholars are not completely clueless about Greek concepts of the physical nature of the underworld; it is consistently described as a gray, sunless land of souls, where the deceased rejoined family members and friends who had preceded them to Hades. At its back existed the "Halls of Hades," where the enthroned death god, Hades, ruled. At his side sat his queen, the goddess Persephone. The Halls of Hades also separated the land of the dead from the realm of Tartarus, a dark, windless, and subterranean place of punishment for the immortals. Guarding the entrance to Tartarus were the three "Hundred-Handers," immortals said to have one hundred arms and fifty heads apiece.

Tartarus and Immortal Imprisonment

In describing the depths of Tartarus, the ancient Greek storyteller Hesiod tells that a bronze anvil, if dropped from heaven, would take ten days to reach earth and then another ten to arrive at Tartarus. This terrible pit was so dark, says Hesiod, that it is as if "night is poured around it in three rows like a collar round the neck, while above it grows the roots of the earth and the unharvested sea."[14] The history of Tartarus and how the first immortals, called Titans, came to be confined there begins with Zeus's father, Cronus, who would later be imprisoned.

Before Zeus's birth, even before the creation of humankind, the earth and the heavens were ruled by the Titan Cronus. During his reign, Cronus feared the strongest of his many brothers: the three Hundred-Handers for their great strength and the three Cyclopes for their ability to manufacture weapons. To prevent these powerful siblings from challenging his power, Cronus confined them to the darkness of Tartarus. The cruel Cronus also worried that one of his children might challenge him, so every time Rhea, his wife, gave birth, he swallowed the baby whole. Upset by the loss of her children, Rhea devised a plan to outwit

31

her husband. When Zeus was born, Rhea wrapped a rock in a blanket and allowed her husband to think it was the new baby. Cronus grabbed the bundle, swallowed it, and believed he had eliminated another son. Meanwhile, Zeus was raised in secret until he was old enough to lead a rebellion.

When Zeus came of age, Rhea again tricked Cronus, this time into vomiting up the couple's other children, now fully grown. Secretly, Zeus called a meeting to explain his plans for conquering Cronus. He invited not only his regurgitated brothers and sisters but also the gods who held office under Cronus. So, to insure the help of the other gods, Zeus promised that, when he took control from his father, no gods would lose their previously held positions; furthermore, he swore that those gods who were excluded from positions of power by Cronus would be allowed to wield influence over the affairs of the gods.

Zeus and his followers fought against Cronus and his allies, but neither side could gain the upper hand. Then, as second century A.D. historian Apollodorus describes,

> When they had been fighting for ten years, Rhea prophesized that the victory would go to Zeus if he took as his

allies those who had been hurled down to Tartaros [Tartarus]. So he killed Campe, who was guarding them, and set [the Cyclopes and the Hundred-Handers] free. And the Cyclopes then gave Zeus thunder, lightning and the thunderbolt, and they gave a helmet to Hades, and a trident to Poseidon. Armed with these weapons [and with the aid of the Hundred-

The gods fight the Titans for supremacy of the world. Eventually the gods won and imprisoned the Titans in the underworld.

Handers], they overpowered the Titans, and imprisoned them in Tartaros, appointing the Hundred-Handers as their guards.[15]

With the Titans banished to the underworld, Zeus and his two brothers divided the kingdom of Cronus among themselves. Zeus became the ruler of the heavens, Poseidon was given the sea, and Hades received the earth and that which was inside—the underworld itself.

Thereafter, within the underworld but outside Tartarus, Hades established his fortress. When the human race was created, the living were given residence on earth, the neutral land outside the underworld, while Hades became the domain of the dead.

Hades and the Earth

Hades was associated not only with the death of mortals, but also with the death of the earth each winter. How the underworld came to be associated with the seasons is explained by Hades' kidnapping of Persephone, a daughter of Zeus, to be his bride.

Once settled in the underworld, Hades secured the permission of Zeus to abduct and marry Persephone. One day, while Persephone was picking flowers with her friends, a flower of indescribable beauty grew in her path. When Persephone reached to pick the flower, Hades emerged from the underworld and, grabbing her about the waist, kidnapped her. In a panic, she called aloud, and her cries echoed through the earth even as Hades carried her to his underworld fortress. Her final calls were heard by her mother, Demeter, the goddess of the seasons. To protest the kidnapping, Demeter went into isolation and hid all the seeds of the earth. As a result, humankind began to starve.

Because of Demeter's refusal to be placated, the other gods begged Hades to release Persephone. Eventually Hades acquiesced, but not before reminding Persephone of the advantages of being his wife. He said to her:

> Go on, Persephone, back to your mother in her black veil, go with a kind heart. Do not despair too much: it is useless. As a husband, I will not be unworthy of you among the gods: I am the brother of your father, Zeus. When you're here, you will reign over everyone who lives and moves, and you will have the greatest honors among the gods. And there will be eternal punishment for those who do you wrong and who do not appease your heart piously with sacrifices and great gifts.[16]

As final insurance that Persephone would return to him, Hades fed her some pomegranate seeds; anyone who ate the pomegranate, the food of the underworld, could never return permanently to the world of the living. When Demeter

Castor and Polydeuces

The twin brothers Castor and Polydeuces are unique in ancient Greek mythology as they represent both the immortality of the gods and the plight of humankind in Hades. According to legend, the two brothers were inseparable companions. However, in an ambush orchestrated by their enemies, Castor was killed, but Polydeuces was saved by Zeus and offered the gift of immortality. Polydeuces, though, wanted his brother to share his gift and was unwilling to accept immortality while Castor remained in the land of the dead. Hades, however, was not willing to relinquish the dead twin's soul. Consequently, Zeus struck a bargain between Polydeuces and Hades, deciding that both brothers would live forever, but not in the way Polydeuces had hoped. Instead, for half the year Polydeuces would reside in heaven and Castor in the underworld, while during the other half, the brothers would switch places. Thus Polydeuces succeeded in gaining immortality for his twin but could no longer enjoy his company.

learned that her daughter had eaten the seeds, she was horrified, but Zeus arranged a compromise between Hades and Demeter: Persephone would spend three months of the year in the underworld as Hades' queen; during the rest of the year, Persephone would reside with her mother. Accordingly, the ancient Greeks believed that every winter, Demeter mourned the absence of her daughter and withdrew her gift of fertility to the earth.

Journey to the Underworld

Unlike the immortal Persephone, however, dead mortals were never allowed to return to the land of the living. According to Greek legend, Hermes, Charon, and Cerberus escorted the spirits of the dead to the underworld where they were expected to spend eternity. As Homer describes in a passage from his tale *The Odyssey:*

> He [Hermes] waved them on, all squeaking
> as bats will in a cavern's underworld,
> all flitting, flitting criss-cross in the dark
> if one falls and the rock-hung chain is broken.
> So with faint cries the shades [souls of the dead] trailed after Hermes,
> pure Deliverer.
>
> He led them down dank ways,
> over gray Ocean tides, the Snowy Rock,
> past shores of Dream and narrows

of the sunset,
in swift flight to where the dead
inhabit
wastes . . . at the world's end.[17]

For the living, the journey to the underworld was both difficult and perilous. One of the few mortals to make the journey to Hades' land was the mythic hero and fabled singer Orpheus. Orpheus's journey to the underworld is one of the most significant myths of ancient Greece. He sought to revive his wife, Eurydice,

who was killed by a snakebite to the foot. And it is through the story of his journey to the underworld that the ancient Greeks were able to discuss both the terrors of the paths the dead took to the underworld and the ultimate futility of even the most courageous, resourceful attempts to revive the deceased.

Leaving his home, Orpheus journeyed overland until he arrived at a cave in the land of Tænarus. Entering the cave, he made his way down the paths reserved for the dead until he arrived at the dark waters of the Styx. On its bank waited Charon, the ferryman, who is described in *Bulfinch's Mythology* as an "old and squalid, but strong and vigorous" immortal who transports "passengers of all kinds in his boat, magnanimous heroes, boys and unmarried girls, as numerous as the leaves that fall at autumn."[18] Bravely, Orpheus boarded the ferry and took a seat among the spirits of the dead.

On the opposite shore, Orpheus passed Cerberus, the guardian of the gates of Hades whom an ancient Greek writer, Apollodorus, describes as having "three dogs' heads, the tail of a dragon, and on his back, the heads of all kinds of

Charon ferries souls across the River Styx. The hero Orpheus met Charon on his journey to the underworld.

The three-headed dog Cerberus guards the entrance to the underworld.

snakes."[19] Orpheus then continued his descent, negotiating steep caverns that at last opened onto the plains of the underworld, facing the domain of Hades.

Orpheus Pleads for His Bride

Orpheus soon traveled to the great palace of Hades where he faced the death god and Persephone, his queen. The talented Orpheus, a son of Apollo, sang magnificently of Eurydice, and of his love for his deceased bride as he begged for her return:

> O deities of the underworld, to whom all we who live must come, hear my words, for they are true. I come not to spy out the secrets of Tartarus, nor to try my strength against the three-headed dog with snaky hair who guards the entrance. I come to seek my wife, whose opening years the poisonous viper's fang had brought to an untimely end. Love has led me here. Love, a god all powerful with us who dwell on earth, and, if old traditions say true, not less so here. I implore you by these abodes full of terror, these realms of silence and uncreated things, unite again the thread of Eurydice's life. We are all destined to you, and sooner or later must pass to your domain. She too, when she shall have filled her term of life,

will rightly be yours. But till then, grant her to me, I beseech you.[20]

The ghosts and other denizens of the underworld wept at the song. Even Hades and his queen were overcome. Consequently, Hades relented and called Eurydice forth. As Bulfinch continues the story,

She came from the newly arrived ghosts, limping with her wounded foot. Orpheus was permitted to take her away on one condition, that he should not look at her till they should have reached the upper air. Under this condition they proceeded on their way, he leading, she

Orpheus (right) breaks his vow and turns to look at Eurydice, who is instantly dragged back to the underworld.

following, through the passages dark and steep.[21]

Just as they were about to emerge into the land of the living, though, Orpheus forgot Hades' command and looked behind him. Instantly, Eurydice was borne away, back to the halls of the dead. In despair, Orpheus tried to chase after her, but Charon refused to take him back across the Styx. Orpheus, like all others, would have to wait for his own death to be reunited with his bride.

The Fates of the Dead

Like Orpheus, Odysseus, the wandering hero of Homer's *Odyssey*, also had to journey to the land of the dead. However, he sought not a loved one but the ghost of the seer Tiresias. Odysseus believed the gods were keeping him from his kingdom in Ithaca, and he hoped Tiresias could tell him why. During the course of his adventure, Odysseus spoke with a number of different ghosts, who expressed concerns about life and death in ways typical of the understanding of the time.

After many days of travel, Odysseus arrived at the end of the sea, where the rivers of the underworld met. He ventured forth into the grove of Persephone, an entrance to Hades' realm. There, he dug a pit into which he poured the blood of two just-slaughtered rams. Attracted by the warm blood, the souls of the dead swarmed around him. One at a time, Odysseus allowed the ghosts to drink of

the blood, which empowered them to speak with the living.

To Odysseus's surprise, the first ghost to approach was that of his comrade, Elpenor, who had died early in the trip to the underworld. Odysseus asked how Elpenor could have arrived first in the land of the dead, as they had been traveling together. In response, Elpenor explained that as a rule, the deceased reached the underworld by a much quicker path than that available to the living. He then told Odysseus that his body rested unattended and unburied and demanded that his former leader return to the corpse and perform the burial honors befitting a fallen warrior; only then would Elpenor be serene in his death.

Next, Odysseus spoke with his mother, Anticleia, of whose death he had not been aware. After taking her turn at the spilt blood, Anticleia attributed her death to loneliness for Odysseus. Overcome by the sight of his dead mother, Odysseus sought to embrace her. Three times, he tried, but each attempt failed as his hands passed through the ghost's insubstantial form. Distraught, he wondered aloud if he were not the victim of some trick or illusion. But Anticleia explained:

> All mortals meet this judgment [become a ghost] when they die.
> No flesh and bone are here, none bound by sinew,

since the bright-hearted pyre
consumed them down—
the white bones long examinate
[no longer moving]—to ash;
dream-like the soul flies, insubstantial.[22]

With the knowledge that his mother was
truly beyond his reach in the land of the
dead, Odysseus bid Anticleia farewell
and allowed her to depart.

Pride and Regret in Death

Two others with whom Odysseus had the
opportunity to speak were the ghosts of his
former comrade Achilles and the dead king
of Greece, Agamemnon. In the course of
their conversations, Odysseus learns of the

eternal pride of Achilles, his reward in
death, and the eternal punishment of pain
and bitterness of Agamemnon.

Agamemnon was the first to approach,
and Odysseus wept upon seeing the once
powerful warrior-king reduced to a frail
and insubstantial ghost. At once, Odysseus
asked his former friend how he had met his
end. Sadly, Agamemnon related that he
and his men had been betrayed and killed
by his wife, Clytemnestra, and her lover,
Aegisthus, during a dinner celebrating his
return from the Trojan War, a vicious ten-
year struggle in which Agamemnon, with
the assistance of Odysseus, had triumphed.
He says:

It was Aigísthos [Aegisthus] who
designed my death,

The hero Odysseus (pictured) traveled to the underworld seeking information from the seer Tiresias.

The Furies

Although the ancient Greeks believed that the majority of humankind was not punished in the afterlife, they did believe that otherworldly forces existed to chastise humans who committed crimes for which they would never have otherwise been caught. These forces, called the Furies, came from the underworld and were considered to be the avenging spirits of the land of the dead. Although the number of Furies originally varied considerably, eventually there came to be only three: Alecto, Megaera, and Tisiphone.

One of the best known tales involving the Furies is that of Orestes, who had killed his mother; the slaughter of a mother by her son was taboo in ancient Greece for any reason. To punish Orestes, the Furies chased him throughout Greece until he was nearly overcome by insanity. Eventually, he was granted a reprieve after the gods ascertained that he had been punished enough.

he and my heartless wife, and
    killed me, after
feeding me, like an ox felled at
    the trough.
That was my miserable end—
    and with me
my fellows butchered . . .

In your day
you have seen men, and hun-
    dreds, die in war,
in the bloody press, or downed in
    single combat,
but these were murders you
    would catch your breath at:
think of us fallen, all our throats
    cut, winebowl
brimming, tables laden on every
    side,
while blood ran smoking over
    the white floor.[23]

When Agamemnon returned to the underworld, he went away in bitterness and anger for all eternity because he was haunted by the betrayal and dishonor of his death.

Achilles, one of the heroes of the Trojan War, was one of the last ghosts to approach. He strode confidently up to Odysseus and said that his only concern was for his son, Neoptolemus, and how he had fared without a father. Odysseus responded that Neoptolemus had fought well after the death of his father:

And when we formed against
    the Trojan line [the enemy]
he never hung back in the mass,
    but ranged
far forward of his troops—no
    man could touch him
for gallantry [bravery]. Aye, scores

went down before him
in hard fights man to man.[24]

On hearing that his son had fought bravely, Achilles proudly left Odysseus's company, glad to know that Neoptolemus, too, had become a great warrior. Achilles could now be content in the land of the dead.

Following these encounters, the lingering Odysseus grew fearful of the other spirits who milled around him wanting to taste the rams' blood, and hurriedly departed. Like Orpheus before him, Odysseus had come to understand the inevitability and permanence of death. Further, the contrasting fates of his two deceased comrades, Agamemnon's bitterness and Achilles' contentedness, showed Odysseus that what happens in life determines one's everlasting fate in the underworld.

The Celts: The Fairiefolk of the Afterlife

Chapter Three

Much of Celtic literature describes the location of that culture's afterlife as a set of islands located far to the west of contemporary Ireland. The Celts believed that the land of the dead was occupied not only by the ghosts of human beings but also by the Celtic gods and a whole race of otherworld peoples, known as the fairiefolk or Sidhe, which were thought to be intimately connected with the death of mortals.

A complete understanding of the mythology of the Celtic people, however, is impossible. For, although as early as 1200 B.C. the Celts inhabited much of Europe, including present-day Germany, Spain, France, England, and Ireland, it is difficult to discuss all aspects of their mythology because little Celtic literature has been preserved. This in turn is because the Celtic peoples did not write down their own tales; instead they transmitted the culture's legends orally; that is, older generations taught the younger Celts by word of mouth.

The Celtic literature that was recorded consists of the myths of the Celts who preserved their culture the longest, namely the tribes of Ireland and Wales. These stories were eventually transcribed by Christian monks who visited Wales during the second century and Ireland during the seventh. The monks' records are incomplete, however, for many manuscripts were destroyed in the course of successive invasions by Romans, Vikings, Saxons, and Normans between the years 100 and 1300. As a result, what scholars have learned of the Celtic land of the dead comes primarily from a few remaining fragments of Celtic tales from Europe's northern islands.

Tír na nÓg

Called Tír na nÓg, the afterlife of the Celts was actually a mix of many realms. As the land of the dead, it was a place in

This stone head from the ancient Celtic culture was found in southwestern England.

which the deceased enjoyed new, relatively carefree lives. Yet Tír na nÓg was also a complex place in which the ghosts of men existed in an environment of magic and wonder. As such, Tír na nÓg had a variety of features and purposes within Celtic mythology. As author Proinsias MacCana explains in *Celtic Mythology*:

> The otherworld [Tír na nÓg] . . . is a changing scene of many phases . . . where sickness and decay are unknown. It is a land of . . . innocence where the pleasures of love are untainted by guilt. Its women are numerous and beautiful and they alone people some of its regions, so that then it becomes literally "The Land of Women." . . . It is filled with enchanting music from bright-plumaged [feathered] birds, from the swaying branches of the otherworld tree, from instruments which sound without being played and from the very stones. And it has abundance of exquisite food and drink, and magic vessels of inexhaustible plenty. . . . This world transcends the limitations of human time; the mortal returning from a visit there may suddenly become aged and decrepit on contact with the material world, or he may

simply dissolve into dust. . . . It [Tír na nÓg] may be situated under the ground or under the sea; it may be in distant islands.[25]

Residents of the Afterlife

Perhaps the most important magical component of the Celtic otherworld was its supernatural residents, called the Sidhe. According to Irish legend, the Sidhe were originally called the Tuatha Dé Danann, meaning the people of the goddess Dana. When the Celts arrived in Ireland, they sought to claim the island for themselves; consequently, the Sidhe and the Celts warred. However, neither side was able to gain a distinct advantage. As a result, the two sides developed a compromise. The Sidhe would occupy the otherworld which could not be seen by living men, and the Celts would occupy the physical realm of the mortals.

The Sidhe's otherworld also included islands to the west of Ireland and operated as the afterlife for the Celtic peoples. As a consequence, the Sidhe were intimately involved with the fate of mortal men. The Sidhe, for example, watched over the Irish hero Cuchulain and, in his final moments, they provided magical signs telling him he was about to die. The Sidhe also affected the lives of living people by exerting their otherworldly influence in human affairs. The best known example of this is the saga of Bran mac Febal, who journeys into the Sidhe's world while still alive and glimpses the Celtic afterlife. Last, the Sidhe were often seen as spiritual guardians of deserving, often heroic, mortals. The Celtic-Welsh tale of King Arthur, for instance, involves transporting the gravely injured monarch to the otherworld just as he was about to die. In this way, the Celts believed that King Arthur would be allowed to rest, heal his wounds, and be ready at some point to return to reclaim his kingship over Britain.

Warnings of the Sidhe

Probably the best known of the Celtic-Irish heroes is Cuchulain (or Cù Chulainn), a warrior so successful that he often single-handedly defeated entire armies in combat. However, despite his supernatural valor and warring abilities, even the mighty Cuchulain could not defeat his own mortality; Cuchulain, like all humans, was destined to die. The events leading to the death of Cuchulain were full of omens, or supernatural signs, provided by the Sidhe, in an effort to inform the hero of his impending doom. Thus, because of the influence the Sidhe had on the land of the living, Cuchulain knew even before he arrived at the site of his final battle that he was headed toward his death.

The omens that foretold Cuchulain's demise began just before he set out on his fated last adventure against the army of Maeve, a warrior queen. Before embarking, Cuchulain stopped at the house of his mother, Dechtire, to bid her farewell. As was Celtic custom, Dechtire poured her son a mug of wine. But when Cuchulain started to drink, he discovered that the mug was filled with blood. As Irish mythologian Lady Gregory recounts: "when he took the vessel [mug] in his hand, it was red blood that was in it. 'My grief!' he said, 'my mother Dechtire . . . you yourself offer me a drink of blood.' Then she filled

Cuchulain (on horseback) received numerous signs from the Sidhe predicting his death.

Julius Caesar Comments on the Celts

Roman commander Julius Caesar encountered Celts when he conquered the region of Gaul [modern-day France]. In recording his impressions of the Celtic peoples, Caesar included descriptions of their burial practices. As quoted in Miranda J. Green's *The Gods of the Celts*, Caesar wrote:

Although Gaul is not a rich country, funerals there are splendid and costly. Everything the dead man is thought to have been fond of [in life] is put on the pyre [a large funeral fire], including even animals. Not long ago [in modern terms, several thousand years ago] slaves and dependents known to have been their master's favorites were buried with them [their masters] at the end of the funeral.

Julius Caesar, the Roman leader who conquered Gaul.

the vessel a second, and a third time, and each time when she gave it to him, there was nothing in it but blood."[26]

Eventually, Cuchulain realized the significance of the blood. It was an omen provided by the Sidhe indicating that he would die in his next battle. Despite the warning, Cuchulain refused to be deterred from the fight. Lady Gregory recounts the legend:

Then anger came on Cuchulain, and he dashed the vessel against a rock, and broke it, and he said:

"The fault is not in yourself, my mother Dechtire, but my luck is turned against me, and my life is near its end, and I will not come back alive this time from facing the men of Ireland [Maeve's army]." Then Dechtire tried hard to persuade him to go back and to wait till he would have the help of Conall [Cuchulain's cousin, due to arrive in a few days]. "I will not wait," he said, "for anything you can say; for I would not give up my great name and my courage for all the riches of the world. And from the day I first took arms till this day, I have never drawn back from a fight or a battle. And it is not now I will begin to draw back," he said, "for a great name outlasts life."[27]

A Second Omen

Shortly thereafter, Cuchulain left the house of his mother in the company of his adviser, the elderly Cathbad. At the edge of a river, the two men saw a woman of the Sidhe, vainly trying to rinse blood from Cuchulain's clothes. Lady Gregory takes up the story:

There they saw a young girl, thin and white-skinned and having yellow hair, washing and ever washing, and wringing out clothing that was stained crimson red, and she crying and keening all the time.

"[Cuchulain,]" said Cathbad, "do you see what it is that young girl is doing? It is your red clothes she is washing, and crying as she washes, because she knows you are going to your death against Maeve's great army. And take the warning now and turn back again."

"Dear master," said Cuchulain, "you have followed me far enough; for I will not turn back from my vengeance on the men of Ireland that are coming to burn and to destroy my house and my country. And what is it to me, the woman of the Sidhe to be washing red clothing for me? It is not long till there will be clothing enough, and armour and arms, lying soaked in pools of blood, by my own sword and my spear."[28]

Thus, Cuchulain committed himself to the upcoming fight. He rode his chariot into battle where, after slaying many men, he was finally pierced by his own spear, which was thrown back at him by Lugaid, one of the leaders of the forces of Maeve. Grievously wounded and barely alive, Cuchulain strapped himself to a pillar of stone so that he would die standing; his enemies eventually beheaded him.

Having thus shown himself to have lived a heroic life rather than passing his days in fear of death, Cuchulain was rewarded in the afterlife by being allowed to live in the company of the Sidhe.

The Voyage of Bran

Other Celtic heroes did not have to wait until they died to make the journey to the land of the dead. In fact, the otherworld of the Celts was often itself the goal of heroic quests because heroes desired to know what the land of the dead was like before they took up permanent residence there. Perhaps the best-known journey into the land of the Sidhe was made by Bran mac Febal, a Celtic-Irish hero who was invited by one of the Sidhe to journey to the land of the dead.

Bran's adventure to Tír na nÓg began when he took home a silver branch with white blossoms that had appeared next to him as he was sleeping in the countryside. On entering the central room of his fortress, Bran and his men were amazed to see a woman of the Sidhe. As was characteristic of the Sidhe, the otherworldly woman chose to sing to Bran and his followers. She sang of the beauty and charm of the afterlife, which she described as one hundred and fifty islands, all far to the west of Ireland:

> Splendours of every colour glisten
> Throughout the gentle-voiced
>   plains.
> Joy is known, ranked around
>   music . . .
> Unknown is wailing or treachery
> In the familiar cultivated land,
> There is nothing rough or harsh,
> But sweet music striking on the
>   ear. . . .
>
> A beauty of a wondrous land,
> Whose aspects are lovely,
> Whose view is a fair country,
> Incomparable is its haze.[29]

When her song was finished, the lady of the Sidhe stretched out her arm. The silver branch leapt out of Bran's hand and into her own. Then she disappeared.

A Glimpse of the Afterlife

The following day, Bran assembled three companies of nine men each, and together they sailed toward the land about which the lady of the Sidhe had sung. After two days at sea, another representative of the otherworld spoke with Bran and his men. Manannan, the god of the sea, appeared before them in a chariot pulled over the waves by magical horses.

Manannan welcomed Bran's company and then sang of the differences between the otherworld and the realm of the living. For, while Bran and his men saw only the ocean, Manannan told them of the hidden realm which only the residents of the land of the Sidhe could witness:

> What is a clear sea
> For the prowed skiff [boat] in
>   which Bran is,
> That is a happy plain with profu-
>   sion of flowers
> To me from the chariot of two
>   wheels.[30]

Thus, Bran and his men knew that they were nearing the realm of the Sidhe. With the disappearance of the sea god over the horizon, the Celts entered the land of the dead.

Although the land of the Sidhe is described as infinitely vast, Bran and his followers visited only two of its islands. The first one they came to was called the Island of Joy, for all its residents were laughing constantly. Curious, Bran had one of his men take a small boat to the island to speak with the residents. To Bran's surprise, the man joined in the laughter as soon as he landed on the

Celtic Halloween

The Celtic afterlife was not only the place of the dead but also the source of a holiday that is observed in the twenty-first century: Halloween. The origin of Halloween begins with the division of the Celtic year into two halves, winter and summer. The Feast of Samhain marked the change from summer to winter and was celebrated every year on November first. The Celts believed that during Samhain, the barriers between the natural and the supernatural realms disappeared. Divine beings and the spirits of the dead moved freely among humans and interfered in people's affairs. As a result, the first of November became associated with the dead: what they looked like and what they might do to the living if they chose to reveal themselves. Over time, this belief evolved to include the costumes of ghosts and ghouls that are the trademark of Halloween to this day.

Children celebrate the modern holiday Halloween, which is derived from the Celtic Feast of Samhain.

island. Since it appeared that anyone who set foot on the island would lose all desire to return, Bran decided that he had no choice but to leave the man there, to laugh forever.

Sailing farther west, the Celts came to a second island on which hundreds of beautiful women lived in an idyllic lush garden. As Bran's craft approached the Island of Women, one of them called to Bran to come ashore. She threw him a ball of yarn, which Bran caught. Magically, the boat was drawn to shore by the thread of the yarn. When Bran and his men disembarked, they discovered a paradise. Each man enjoyed the company of one of the women. Delicious foods were always available. Indeed, no request the men might make was refused.

Eventually, however, Bran and his men became homesick for Ireland. And, after

what seemed like only a few years, they headed home despite warnings by the women that things would not be the same.

A Failed Trip Home

On arriving back on the coast of Ireland, Bran and his men were challenged by a group of strangers who would not allow them to land their boat. Bran was astonished when the strangers asked him to identify himself, for he had expected to be recognized as a leader of Ireland. Yet even when Bran gave his name, the men declared that they had heard only of a Bran who had lived many years before.

Frustrated by the response, Nechtan, one of Bran's men, jumped from the boat and onto the shore to confront the strangers directly. As soon as his feet touched the island, though, Nechtan

The House of Donn

Although almost all mythologies contain references to a death god, the Celts were unique in believing that their death god, called Donn, had once been a mortal. The Celts believed that Donn, meaning "brown, or dark one," had been one of the original Celts to land on the shores of Ireland; thus he was a common ancestor of all the Celtic people.

In his days as a mortal, Donn had commanded the first Celtic ship to reach Ireland, then the home of the Sidhe. Yet, before setting foot onto the shores of Ireland, Donn was killed by the Sidhe themselves. Having died, he passed into the Celtic otherworld, where he established a new residence called Tech Duinn or the "House of Donn." According to some Celtic legends, Donn then extended an invitation to all his relatives in the land of the living to take up residence in Tech Duinn when they died. Thus, all the Irish Celts were assured of a place to reside within the afterlife.

instantly turned to dust, as if he had been dead for hundreds of years. Although Bran and his men believed they had spent but a few years in the realm of the Sidhe, they came to realize that from the perspective of mortals, they had spent hundreds of years on the Island of Women. Thus Bran learned that time functioned differently in the two realms. No one who had lived among the Sidhe could ever return to the land of the living. To emphasize this point, Bran sang the following words in memory of his fallen comrade:

> For Collbran's son [Nechtan],
>   great was the folly
> To lift his hand against age,
> Without any one casting a wave
>   of pure water
> Over Nechtan, Collbran's son.[31]

Still speaking from the boat, Bran told the people on the shore of his adventures so that the stories could be written down for future generations. Afterward, Bran and his company departed without having set foot on their native land. The magical powers of the Celtic otherworld were so strong that the mortals had no choice but to return to the land of the Sidhe.

A Celtic King Arthur

Despite the Bran legend, the land of the Sidhe was not always viewed as a place from which mortals never returned. It was also thought to be a place in which the greatest Celtic heroes could be restored to health. One of the most famous mortals

King Arthur was a mythical British ruler. According to Celtic legend, Arthur will someday return from the afterlife to reclaim the throne.

who journeyed to the otherworld for healing was the legendary King Arthur, a mythical ruler of fifth-century Britain.

Many of the tales of King Arthur originated in Celtic Wales, located in western Britain. The most popular of these stories is that of the death of the king and his passing over to the Isle of Avalon, the Welsh equivalent of the Celtic-Irish otherworld. However, unlike Cuchulain or Bran, King Arthur, it was believed, would someday return from his passage into the afterlife, to reclaim the British throne.

After many years of heroism, King Arthur and his knights engaged in one last battle against the forces of Arthur's nephew, Mordred, who wanted to take over the British throne. This final battle, called the Battle of Camlann, was so horrific that nearly all the men on both sides were killed. Finally, King Arthur and Mordred met face to face on the battlefield. King Arthur gripped his spear in both hands and charged at his nephew. Although Arthur ran the younger man through, before dying, Mordred used his sword to pierce Arthur's skull.

Fatally wounded, Arthur was found by his only surviving knight, Sir Bedivere. At the King's command, Sir Bedivere threw Excalibur, Arthur's magical sword, into the ocean. Just as the sword was about to strike the surface of the water, though, a woman's arm emerged from the waves. As Bulfinch relates: "And there came an arm and hand out of the water, and met it [the sword], and caught it, and shook it thrice [three times] and brandished it [waved it menacingly], and then vanished away the hand with the sword in the water."[32] Because the sword had been initially given to King Arthur by the Sidhe in honor of his kingship, the return of the sword communicated to the residents of the Celtic afterlife that King Arthur was fatally wounded and therefore in need of their assistance.

The sword Excalibur rises from the water, alerting the residents of the afterlife that Arthur has been wounded and needs their help.

A Possible Return

When Sir Bedivere informed King Arthur of the hand that had retrieved his sword, Arthur knew

King Arthur (lying down) is transported by ship to the realm of the Sidhe.

that the residents of the afterlife would come for him. Therefore, he had Sir Bedivere assist him to the water's edge. By the time Bedivere and the injured Arthur reached the shore, a boat from the otherworld, the realm of the Sidhe, had already appeared. As Bulfinch describes:

> Then Sir Bedivere took the king on his back, and so went with him to that water-side [the coast]; and when they came there, even fast by [tied to] the bank there rode a little barge [boat] with many fair ladies in it,

and among them was a queen; and all had black hoods, and they wept and shrieked when they saw King Arthur.[33]

King Arthur, though, was not meant to stay in the afterlife forever. Unlike the Celtic heroes of Ireland, he would return from the land of the dead once he had recovered from his wounds. As Bulfinch relates:

> And then they [the black-hooded women] rowed from the land, and Sir Bedivere beheld them go from

him. Then he cried: "Ah, my lord Arthur, will ye leave me here alone among mine enemies?"

"Comfort thyself," said the king, "for in me is no further help; for I will go to the Isle of Avalon [in the otherworld], to heal me of my grievous wound."[34]

Thus, according to the Celtic legend of King Arthur, the fabled king is still alive, yet hidden within the magical realm of the Sidhe.

The Celts believed that Arthur, unlike the deceased Cuchulain or the trapped Bran, could return from the otherworld and reassume his role as king of Britain. However, despite the difference between the myths—that Arthur could return whereas Bran and Cuchulain could not—the tales of the exploits of these heroes have allowed modern scholars to glimpse the afterlife that the Celtic people believed awaited them, an afterlife of magical otherworld beings who interact with mortals while also irreversibly affecting the fates of humans who respond to their calls.

Aztecs: Death, Sacrifice, and Creation

Chapter Four

During the sixteenth century, Spanish soldiers landed on the shores of what is now Mexico and claimed the land as New Spain. Yet the territory was already occupied by the Aztecs, then one of the most sophisticated and developed cultures of the Western Hemisphere. The Spanish conquistadors, however, were less interested in the Aztec culture than in locating gold and jewels; consequently, they murdered the Aztec emperor, looted the country's riches, and in the process destroyed most of the Aztec civilization. As a result, historians have only an incomplete understanding of Aztec beliefs with respect to death.

Using the records that did survive, as well as reports of Spanish soldiers and priests, however, scholars have been able to reconstruct some of the principal religious beliefs of the Aztecs. The role of sacrifice in Aztec society is especially well covered. The Aztecs believed that sacrificial death and the land of the dead—the Aztec underworld—were essential to the continuation of natural cycles. Accordingly, without death and sacrifice, there would never have been any creation at all.

Life Through Death

This relationship between the underworld and creation is a key component in an understanding of Aztec culture. The practices of the Aztecs can be confusing and even revolting to modern sensibilities for the Aztecs routinely offered sacrificial humans to their gods. Spanish explorer Bernal Diaz, who made several visits to Mexico, describes one of the Aztec temples: "There were many diabolical [evil]

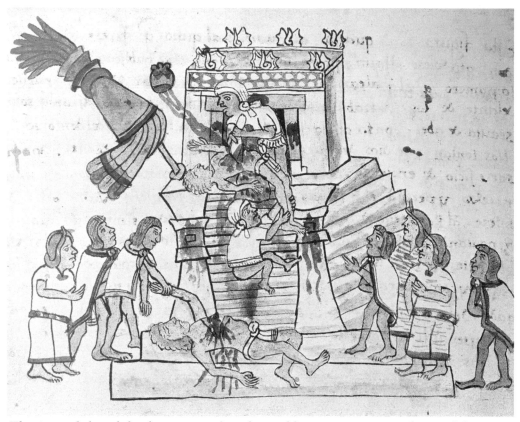

The Aztecs believed that human sacrifice, depicted here, was an essential part of the world's natural cycles.

things . . . and many hearts of Indians . . . and everything was so clotted with blood, and there was so much of it, that I curse the whole of it."³⁵ Yet, for the Aztecs, these sacrificial practices were of the utmost importance because they were believed to be needed to maintain the people's quality of life, and even the natural cycles of life itself.

This importance was expressed in the Aztec word *tlamacehua*, which basically conveys two interrelated meanings: to do penance and to deserve or be worthy of something. The Aztecs believed that in the

beginning, gods had sacrificed themselves to preserve the world. Therefore, the Aztecs felt that, to keep the world going, they also had to sacrifice themselves according to the principles of *tlamacehua*. As historian Miguel León-Portilla explains:

> There was a reciprocal obligation between the gods and humanity. People also had to perform *tlamacehua* . . . including bloody sacrifice of offering human beings. . . . Everything in life—to gain possession of land, water, and food; to

achieve marriage; to have children; and, of course, to approach and satisfy the gods—had to be deserved through penance and sacrifice.[36]

Thus, the most important relationship to the Aztecs was the one between death, and therefore the underworld, and life.

Mictlan, the Aztec Underworld

The Aztecs believed that when an individual died, his or her skeletal corpse descended to the underworld, called Mictlan. In Mictlan, most of the dead were thought to coexist peacefully and uneventfully. However, those who were especially deserving—usually willing sacrificial victims—resided in a place of honor alongside the sun god in the sky.

The fate of the deceased was also intimately connected with creation and life. Indeed, the most important aspect of the underworld was its role in the creation of humankind. The Aztecs believed that the bones of former humans were stored in Mictlan.

When the gods decided to create humanity, they had to send one of their own, the god Quetzalcoatl, into the underworld to retrieve the bones that were waiting there. The tale of Quetzalcloatl's descent into Mictlan and

his retrieval of the bones explained for the Aztecs how life originated; it was born from within the land of the dead.

The relationship between sacrifice and the underworld played vital roles in the Aztec creation myths as well. Both the food and drink that sustain human life were brought into the world by way of destruction and death. Indeed, even the creation of the sun and its movement through the sky required the sacrifice of

An ancient Aztec artist's depiction of Death.

This shell sculpture shows Quetzalcoatl rising from a coyote's mouth. Quetzalcoatl had to travel to the underworld to retrieve the bones of the fourth world.

carried off even its sun. The world of fire was destroyed by a rain of fire. And the fourth world was destroyed by a flood.

All the worlds contained people, but with the creation of each successive world, the people who had lived in the destroyed place were transformed into animals. For instance, the people of the fourth world of water were transformed into fish, and their bones were sent to the underworld under the care of the death god, Mictlantecuhtli. When the gods refashioned the world for the fifth time, they again desired to populate the earth with people. To accomplish this, the Aztecs believed, the bones belonging to the fish-people of the previous world had to be retrieved from Mictlan.

Ometeotl, the parent of all Aztec gods, called on his son Quetzalcoatl to go to the underworld to retrieve the bones from the last creation. Quetzalcoatl promptly agreed, but the task would not be a simple one. Mictlan was dangerous even for the gods because it was the realm of the devious and spiteful Mictlantecuhtli.

After entering the caverns that led to the underworld, Quetzalcoatl journeyed to the heart of Mictlan to speak with Mictlantecuhtli. The sixteenth-century manuscript titled *Leyenda de los soles* gives this account:

the gods and thereafter, according to the Aztecs, the sacrifice of humanity.

Quetzalcoatl Goes to the Underworld

The Aztecs believed that the world in which they lived was actually the fifth world, or "sun," to have existed. Each of the previous worlds corresponded to one of the four elemental forms: earth, wind, fire, or water. Further, each of these earlier worlds had been destroyed by its own element. The world of earth was destroyed by jaguars, a creature the Aztecs regarded as close to the earth and its underworld. The world of wind was destroyed by windstorms, which

Quetzalcoatl went to Mictlan. He approached Mictlantecuhtli . . . at once he spoke to [Mictlantecuhtli]:

"I come in search of the precious bones in your possession. I have come for them."

And Mictlantecuhtli asked of him, "What shall you do with them, Quetzalcoatl?"

And . . . Quetzalcoatl said, "The gods are anxious that someone should inhabit the earth."[37]

Quetzalcoatl

Of all the Aztec gods, perhaps the most important is Quetzalcoatl. Notably, he is the god who retrieves the bones of humans from the underworld, thereby allowing for the creation of more people. But Quetzalcoatl's role as a maker and preserver of life extended beyond the initial creation of humankind.

Quetzalcoatl was believed to exist in the breath of human beings as well as in the wind that brought the storm clouds, and therefore life-giving rain to the Aztecs. Since it was the presence of Quetzalcoatl that created and sustained life, the death of a person, as evidenced by the cessation of breathing, was taken to signify the departure of the god and the end of mortal life.

Mictlantecuhtli, though, did not want to give up the bones because he had no wish for life to resume on earth. However, neither did the god of death want to directly oppose all the other gods, who did want a human population on the fifth world. The god of the underworld therefore decided to trick Quetzalcoatl by agreeing to give up the bones provided Quetzalcoatl could accomplish a seemingly simple task. As author Karl Taube describes in *Aztec and Maya Myths*, however, Mictlantecuhtli thought he had made the job impossible:

[Mictlantecuhtli] tells Quetzalcoatl to travel around his underworld realm four times while sounding a conch shell trumpet. However, instead of a shell trumpet, Mictlantecuhtli gives Quetzalcoatl a simple conch with no holes. Not to be outsmarted, Quetzalcoatl calls upon worms to drill holes in the shell and for bees to enter the trumpet and make it roar.[38]

When Mictlantecuhtli heard the conch being played by Quetzalcoatl throughout the underworld, the death god reluctantly agreed to allow Quetzalcoatl to carry away the bones.

Creation from Death

As Quetzalcoatl was leaving the realm of Mictlantecuhtli, though, the death god changed his mind. He ordered his servants

Mictlantecuhtli, shown here, was the dangerous and spiteful god of death.

zalcoatl fell in it, he stumbled and was frightened by the quail. He fell . . . and the precious bones were scattered. The quail chewed and gnawed them."[39]

Although Quetzalcoatl eventually was able to escape from the pit and retrieve all of the bones, he discovered that some bones had been broken when he fell. The Aztecs used this accident to explain why some people are very tall, some of medium height, and some quite short.

With the bones finally out of the clutches of Mictlantecuhtli and in Quetzalcoatl's possession, it was once again possible to create people. However, further sacrifice, in the form of blood, on the part of the gods was needed. As Taube explains:

> Having escaped the underworld, Quetzalcoatl carries the precious load [of bones] to Tamoanchan, a miraculous place of origin. There the old goddess Cihuacoatl, or Woman Serpent, grinds the bones into a flour-like meal which she places in a special ceramic container. The gods gather around this vessel and shed drops of their blood upon the ground bones, and from the bones of the fish people mixed with the . . . blood of the gods, the present race of humans are born.[40]

Grain and the Underworld

to construct a deep pit on the path Quetzalcoatl would use to return to the realm of the living. As Quetzalcoatl hurried toward the pit, the death god ordered a quail to burst from the bushes at Quetzalcoatl's feet. Startled by the darting bird, Quetzalcoatl stumbled and fell into the hole. The story continues in *Leyenda de los soles:* "The pit having been made, Quet-

Since the earth would again be populated with people, the gods had to provide

The Duties of the Sages

The Aztecs were guided in their spiritual beliefs by their sages, called *tlamatinimeh* which means "those who know something." The *tlamatinimeh* were responsible for all religious sacrifices, including the drawing of their own blood in an effort to appease the demands of the gods. Their religious responsibilities included following the movement of the stars in order to forecast the will of the gods, and writing the sacred texts of the Aztec priesthood. As quoted in Miguel León-Portilla's "Those Made Worthy by Divine Sacrifice: The Faith of Ancient Mexico," the recovered Aztec record called the *Book of Colloquies* explains the *tlamatinimeh*'s multiple social roles.

There are those who guide us . . .
who instruct us
how our gods must be worshiped,
who make offerings,
who burn incense,
those who receive the title of Quetzalcoatl [in honor of their connection to the god, Quetzalcoatl]. . . .
They busy themselves day and night
with the placing of the incense,
with their offering,
with the thorns to draw their blood.
Those who see,
who dedicate themselves to observing
the courses of the stars,
and the movements of the heavens,
and how the night is divided.
Those who read their books,
who recite what they read . . .
they who are in possession of the black and red inks
—of wisdom—
and that which is depicted.
They lead us,
they guide us,
they tell us the way . . .
to them falls
to speak of the gods.

In a sacrificial ritual, two Aztec gladiators fight to the death.

nourishment for their new creations. Therefore, all the gods embarked on separate journeys in an effort to locate a suitable food for people. However, it would be Quetzalcoatl who would discover the secret hiding place of food within the underworld.

On his search for food, Quetzalcoatl spied a red ant carrying a single grain of maize in its mouth. Quetzalcoatl asked the ant where this food had come from. Initially, the ant refused to give away the hiding place of the grain. As Taube explains:

> The ant refuses to tell, but after much bullying agrees to take Quetzalcoatl to the source, Mount Tonacatepel, Mountain of Sustenance. Transforming himself into a black ant, Quetzalcoatl squeezes through the narrow opening and follows the red ant deep into the stony mountain to a chamber [in the underworld] filled with seed and grain. Taking some kernels of maize, Quetzalcoatl returns to Tamoanchan. The gods chew the maize and place the mash in the mouths of the infant humans to give them strength.[41]

The gods then discussed how they might expose the grain Quetzalcoatl had discovered in the underworld hiding place. Eventually, the gods decided that the best option was to break the mountain apart. The gods of rain and lightning launched an assault on the mountain and split it open, causing the release of all the grain contained in the underworld chamber. Then the winds picked the grains up and spread them throughout the fifth world, making them available to humankind.

Death and Pulque

Although the people of the earth would be able to feed themselves, the gods noted that there was little in peoples' lives to give them pleasure. In an effort to remedy this situation, Quetzalcoatl suggested that the gods provide intoxicating drinks to induce the people to dance, sing, and enjoy the life they have been given.

In pursuit of this end, Quetzalcoatl sought a partner. He journeyed skyward to the celestial home of the young virgin goddess Mayahuel, who lived with her grandmother, a *tzitzimime* or star demon, of horrid appearance and fearsome countenance. Taube describes what happened next: "Finding the virgin Mayahuel asleep, Quetzalcoatl wakes her and persuades the goddess to descend with him to earth. There they join themselves into a great forked tree, with Quetzalcoatl as one branch and Mayahuel the other."[42]

When the *tzitzimime* awoke to find her granddaughter missing, the demon became enraged. Calling on all loathsome kin, the grandmother searched frantically for the missing Mayahuel. To the dismay of the gods, the grandmother eventually found the runaway. As Taube recounts:

> The furious *tzitzimime* dive headlong from the sky to the tree

Aztecs dance to honor and celebrate their gods and to entertain themselves. Quetzalcoatl suggested that the gods provide the Aztecs with alcoholic drinks to induce such activity.

where Quetzalcoatl and Mayahuel are hidden. Just as they arrive, the tree splits in half and the two branches crash to the ground. The grandmother *tzitzimime* recognizes the branch of Mayahuel and, savagely tearing it apart, she passes parts of her granddaughter to all the other *tzitzimime* to devour.[43]

The branch that was Quetzalcoatl went unrecognized and therefore untouched by the marauding *tzitzimime*.

Once the *tzitzimime* had returned to the sky, Quetzalcoatl took his own form and collected the gnawed bones of the con-sumed goddess. Sadly, he buried the bones in the earth. From Mayahuel's grave sprang the first maguey plant, the source of pulque, the fermented juice of which gave the Aztecs their traditional alcoholic drink. Thus a primary source of joy for the Aztecs was actually a product of death itself.

The Sacrifice of the Gods

Mayahuel was not the only immortal to sacrifice her life for the happiness of the newly created humans. With the discovery of food and the creation of pulque, the gods had provided much for humankind;

Regions of the Dead

For the Aztecs, the fate of the dead was determined by the manner in which one died, and there were actually three places where the dead might go when their mortal lives were over. Men who were killed in combat or sacrifice and women who died during childbirth were highly esteemed after death, and the Aztecs believed that the gods rewarded these individuals by assigning them to be companions of the sun in the heavens, continuously honored and rewarded. People who died of water-related causes such as drowning or being struck by lightning were believed to be awarded a place in a different kind of paradise; the rain god Tlaloc welcomed these individuals into his garden of pleasure, a paradise in which all of one's desires were satisfied. All other persons retired at death to Mictlan, the Aztec underworld. In this "Region of the Dead," which supposedly lay beneath the earth, the dead were believed to be reunited with family members who had died before them.

yet the world was still sunless and dark. The creation of the god who would be the sun for the fifth world became the most costly of all the gifts of the gods, as each god would ultimately have to sacrifice his own life to bring light to the world.

According to Aztec legend, after the creation of pulque, the gods convened at Teotihuacan, a city located twenty-five miles northeast of today's Mexico City, to discuss the matter of a new sun. Huddling in the darkness, they discussed which god should become the sun god for the new world. As the *Leyenda de los soles* reports:

The gods gathered themselves together and took council among themselves there at Teotihuacan. They spoke; they said among themselves:

"Come hither, O gods! Who will carry the burden? Who will take it upon himself to be the sun, to bring the dawn?"[44]

The first to volunteer, the god Tecuciztecatl, desired the prominence the position of sun god would bring him. But the other gods, offended by this bare-faced bid for personal glory, sought to elect a challenger. They chose the sickly Nanahuatzin because they deemed him most worthy. Unlike the prideful Tecuciztecatl, the feeble Nanahuatzin accepted the nomination with humility, not as an honor but as his duty to the other gods. Thus there were two contenders for the position of the sun god. Yet for either god to become the sun, he would first have to sacrifice himself: only through a god's death could the sun be created.

Accordingly, a huge sacrificial fire was built between the two hills of the city, Teotihuacan. Tecuciztecatl and Nanahuatzin poised themselves on the top of one of the hills, known to the Aztecs as the hills of the sun and the moon. In preparation for self-sacrifice, Tecuciztecatl burned the finest wares he could muster because he believed that a demonstration of wealth meant he was the more worthy contender. Thus, instead of the traditional Aztec offering of fir boughs, Tecuciztecatl offered the plumes of quetzal birds, sacred to the Aztecs because Quetzalcoatl was often depicted as a plumed serpent. He also offered balls of gold instead of the traditional bundles of grass. And in place of maguey spines tipped with his own blood, Tecuciztecatl offered awls made of jade tipped with red coral.

Nanahuatzin's offerings were of a much humbler sort. Instead of the fir boughs or grass bundles, Nanahuatzin offered only bundles of reeds. He offered maguey spines smeared with his own blood. Further, he picked the scabs from his diseased body and burned them as incense.

Finally, at midnight on the fourth day, the two gods prepared for the final sacrifice. They dressed in new clothes, Tecuciztecatl in his best finery and Nanahuatzin in simple clothing made of paper. When the candidates signaled that they were ready, all the other gods appeared around the fire which, having burned for four days, was intensely hot with flames still leaping from the red coals. Then the gods called on the proud Tecuciztecatl to sacrifice himself by giving over his life to death. As Taube describes:

> Standing along both sides of the fire, the gods call for Tecuciztecatl to jump into the flames. Tecuciztecatl runs towards the pyre, but the heat and searing flames terrify him and he falters. Once more he tries, and again he is halted by the fire. Four times he runs towards the fire, but every time, he wavers and stops.[45]

Convinced that Tecuciztecatl could not live up to his earlier pledge, the gods turned their attentions to the patient Nanahuatzin. In unison, the gods called on Nanahuatzin to offer himself to death. Immediately, Nanahuatzin ran toward the fire and leapt. As is described in the *Leyenda de los soles*:

> Nanahuatzin, daring all at once, determined—resolved—hardened his heart, and shut firmly his eyes. He had no fear; he did not stop short; he did not falter in fright; he did not turn back. All at once he quickly threw and cast himself into the fire; once and for all he went. Thereupon he burned; his body crackled and sizzled.[46]

Humbled by the heroic and resolute fashion with which Nanahuatzin had sacrificed his life, Tecuciztecatl ran after him, finally casting himself into the flames.

Book of Paintings

Because the Aztecs believed that the gods had sacrificed themselves to allow for the creation of humankind, the people considered themselves to be very fortunate and blessed. One way the Aztecs used to express their gratitude to the gods was poetry. One such poem, normally attributed to the Aztec sage Nezahualcoyotl (1402–1472), praises the work of the gods by comparing the creation of all creatures to a book of paintings made by the gods themselves. The poem, quoted in Miguel León-Portilla's article, "Those Made Worthy by Divine Sacrifice: The Faith of Ancient Mexico," reads as follows:

With flowers you [the gods] inscribe,
Giver of Life,
with songs you give color [liveliness] to
those who will live on the earth.

Later you destroy
eagles and tigers,
we [humanity] live only in your book of paintings
here, on the earth.

You delineate [portray]
all that is friendship,
brotherhood, and nobility.

You give shading [contrast and shadow] to
those who will live on the earth. . . .
We live only in your book of paintings
here, on the earth.

Death and Resurrection

Once the fire had consumed the bodies of Nanahuatzin and Tecuciztecatl, the rest of the gods waited impatiently. They knew that the death of the two gods would allow for their rebirth as sun gods, but none knew exactly how this would happen.

In time, however, the horizon around the earth began to redden with the fifth world's first dawn. Rising in the east, Nanahuatzin emerged. He was an altogether different god. No longer humble or sickly, Nanahuatzin had been reborn as the sun god Tonatiuh, and therefore the sun itself. As the *Leyenda de los soles* relates: "And when the sun came to rise, when he burst forth, he appeared to be red; he kept swaying from side to side. It was impossible to look him in the face; he blinded one with his light."[47]

Yet Nanahuatzin was not the only god to emerge in the eastern skies. Tecuciztecatl had also jumped into the fire; as a result, he too was reborn in the form of a sun. So similar were the two gods in their luminous appearance, however, that the other gods feared the world would be too bright. Therefore, one of the gods scooped up a rabbit, which he flung into the face of Tecuciztecatl. Wounded by the rabbit, Tecuciztecatl could no longer shine as brightly as his old rival Nanahuatzin, now Tonatiuh. Thereafter, the vain and prideful god became the moon, less important than the sun. And when the moon is full, the image of the rabbit can still be seen on its face.

Tonatiuh, in his new state, however, demonstrated a new arrogance. After ascending to the sky, he refused to move in the arc that would allow for the passing of the day. The other gods entreated him to begin moving, but Tonatiuh refused, saying that he would not allow for the passing of the day unless all the other gods, with the exception of Quetzalcoatl, sacrificed themselves in his honor. Eventually, the gods agreed. As Taube explains:

Methodically, one by one, Quetzalcoatl cuts the hearts out of each god with a sacrificial

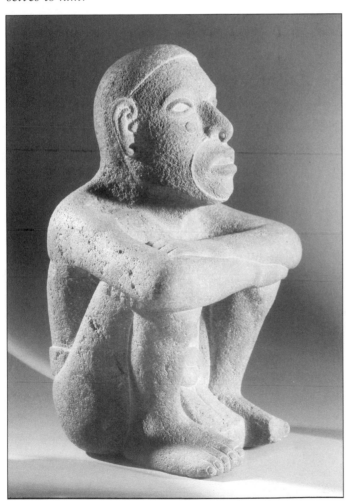

Tonatiuh, the sun god, was arrogant and refused to move across the sky unless other gods sacrificed themselves to him.

blade. The mantles and finery of the dead gods are wrapped up in sacred bundles, the form in which they are then worshiped by people. From the slaying of the gods at Teotihuacan, the Sun of Motion, Nahui Ollin [the new name of Tonatiuh], is created. Just as the gods had to sacrifice themselves, so humans must supply their own hearts and blood to ensure that the fifth sun continues to move in its path.[48]

Penance and Worthiness

In this way, the gods demonstrated their willingness to sacrifice themselves to complete the world they had created. Their behavior fitted perfectly with the Aztec belief in *tlamacehua* (penance and worthiness). Each of the culture's stories helps

Like the gods before them, Aztecs sacrifice a human heart to Tonatiuh so he will continue to make his daily journey across the sky.

explain the importance of *tlamacehua* and the importance of death. According to León-Portilla:

> The key concept of *tlamacehua* denotes the primary and essential relation [relationship] human beings have with their gods. These, through their own penance and sacrifice, deserved—brought into existence—human beings. The gods did this because they were in need of someone who would worship them, someone who could provide them, the gods, with sustenance so that they could continue to foster life on earth. They could not, however, do this without human cooperation.[49]

The Aztecs believed in the power of death as a transformer of life. For example, they held that the remains of the dead had been retrieved from the underworld to become the Aztec people themselves. Like those bones, or the gift of food and drink, the death of the gods was an act of sacrifice that provided the world for humankind. Sacrifice of mortals, then, was also necessary to maintain the powers of creation and life.

Natives of North America: In Death as in Life

Chapter Five

Despite the many similarities between the various native tribes of North America, there is no single set of myths that can be ascribed to all of them. Thus, whenever experts provide general commentary regarding Native American beliefs, they can do no more than isolate similar approaches to lifestyle; the different gods and spiritual practices of each tradition are too numerous to be treated in any but the most comprehensive, multivolume texts. One cultural similarity is that Native Americans believed the afterlife was for the most part identical to the land of the living. And, since the inhabitants of both worlds lived virtually the same lifestyle, Native Americans also thought the land of the living was accessible to the ghosts of the spirit world, and the land of the dead was accessible to the living humans.

Myths a Part of Everyday Life

In all the Native American languages—more than 250 of which are still spoken today—there is no word for "religion." Instead, particularly before the arrival of Europeans, the belief systems of Native Americans were part of everyday life. For example, on a daily basis, they performed songs and dances that recounted or re-enacted their mythology. These performances celebrated the unity between the people and the natural world. The elements of the natural world—Sun, Moon, Stars, the Animals, Corn, and ancestors, for example—were revered and considered to be spiritual forces that influenced the life and death of humans.

This belief created a sense of spirituality that led many tribes to suggest that humans were destined to die, as were elements of the natural world. The inevitability of death, they contended, was a decision made by the gods or other creative forces. Native Americans believed that humankind could have been immortal, yet the controlling powers (the gods) decided—at the last minute—that humankind was to die after all. As a result, the land of the dead was thought simply to be the humans' next residence prepared by the gods in recompense for death. In that residence, the spiritual and cultural practices of the living continued. As James L. Haley explains with respect to the beliefs of the Apache:

> All Apaches apparently shared the belief that life was more meaningful in the hereafter, and that ceremonies that occurred on

earth occurred also on the other side. A person spent his time [in the afterlife] at what he was best at on earth, and the old life of hunting, gathering, and raiding were followed in joy [were joyfully resumed].[50]

The way living humans interacted with the souls of the dead and the significance of that interaction varied considerably, however. For some tribes, such as the Pawnee, the appearance of ghosts in the world of the living served the purpose of communicating that a land of the dead must exist. The Cherokee, on the other hand, maintained that the land of the dead had been initially accessible to humans only to be closed at a later date, a

In this nineteenth-century painting, Native Americans dance as a way of communicating with their gods.

Native Americans decorated their warrior cloaks (like the one pictured here) with illustrations of gods and spirits.

fact that explained the permanence of death. Then there were traditions like that of the Algonquian, which contained tales of living humans who journeyed to the afterlife only to be returned to earth to finish out their mortal lives.

Proof of an Afterlife

Most Native American tribes believed in ghosts. In fact, for the Pawnee, the presence of any ghost meant that life after death was achievable; thus the physical location of the afterlife was relatively unimportant. One Pawnee tale, the leg-

end of the ghost woman, illustrates this idea.

Just as members of one group of Pawnee were supposed to leave their main village on a journey for the annual hunt, a young woman of the tribe died unexpectedly. The Pawnee mourned her loss, dressed the corpse in the girl's finest clothes, and performed the burial ceremony. Then they embarked on the hunt.

Soon the dead girl's fiancé, who had not known of her sudden death, returned to the deserted village after a long journey. Only the girl's spirit was there to greet him, but he did not realize he was seeing a ghost. Author George Grinnell reprises the story:

> [The young man] went back alone into the village. It was empty and silent, but before he reached it, he could see, far off, someone sitting on top of a lodge [village house]. When he came near, he saw that it was the girl he loved. He did not know that she had died, and he wondered to see her there alone, for the time was coming when he would be her husband and she his wife. When she saw him coming, she came down from the top of the lodge and went inside. When he came close to her, he spoke and said, "Why are you alone in the village?" She answered him, "They have gone off on the hunt. I was sulky with my relations [family], and they went off and left me behind."[51]

Upon hearing this, the young man resolved that the couple should marry immediately. To his surprise, however, the girl answered that he would have to wait. The next day, at his insistence, the two departed, intending to join the hunt. Eventually, they overtook the travelers from their village; but the girl refused to enter the camp. Grinnell continues:

> She said, "Now we have arrived, but you must go first to the [camp],

The Native American Soul

Unlike the majority of world mythologies, most Native American traditions maintained that individuals had more than one soul. Most common was the belief in two souls, one that animated the body, and included personality, and a second that existed in and controlled people's dreams. In life, these two souls remained separate, but after death, the two souls joined.

Some tribes, however, believed that each person had more than two souls. For example, the Mandan, a Great Plains tribe, believed that the body possessed four different spirits: a white spirit associated with sage, a plant sacred to the tribe; a light brown spirit associated with the meadowlark; a third spirit whose color was associated with the person's dwelling place; and a fourth black spirit, which was associated with the frightening aspects of ghosts. After death, the white and brown joined together and journeyed to the afterlife, the third spirit stayed with the deceased's homestead, and the black spirit haunted the living.

and prepare a place for me. Where I sleep, let it be behind a curtain. For four days and four nights I must remain behind this curtain. Do not speak of me. Do not mention my name to anyone."[52]

Although he did not understand why his fiancée had imposed these conditions, the young man said he would abide by them and entered the camp alone. However, when he arrived at his lodge, he slipped up and asked another woman to go bring into the camp a girl he had left outside. Curious, the woman asked who the girl was. Remembering his instructions, the young man did not want to speak his fiancée's name, but he inadvertently identified her by saying the names of her parents.

Startled, the woman told the young man that the girl outside could not possibly be the girl of whom he spoke as she had died before the start of the hunt. Still, to put a stop to the young man's repeated requests, the woman did as she was asked. As Grinnell explains:

> When the woman went to look for the girl she could not find her. The girl had disappeared. The young man had disobeyed her and told who she was. She had told him that she must stay behind a curtain for four days and that no one must know who she was. . . . And the girl disappeared because she was a ghost.[53]

Because the young woman's spirit had been able to appear as if in human form, the Pawnee believed that an afterlife must exist. The end of the tale makes this clear. According to the story, that same night the young man died in his sleep. Thus, the people were convinced that there must be an afterlife, and the young man, in his death, was believed to be reunited with his betrothed.

The Permanence of Death

Unlike the Pawnee tale of a ghost who appears to the living, legends of other tribes discuss journeys of the living to the land of the dead. Cherokee tradition, for instance, contends that humankind originally had been empowered to travel to the afterlife to bring back those who had died. The first people, however, made a mistake in the retrieval of the first soul, the daughter of the Sun. As a consequence, death became a permanent condition that awaited all Cherokee.

According to the legend, the Sun, an old lady, lived just beyond the earth's horizon; her daughter lived in the middle of the sky, directly above the earth. Every day, as the Sun made her way to the highest point of the sky, she would visit her daughter and sometimes her brother, the Moon.

One day, the Sun mentioned to the Moon that she was insulted by the facial expressions people made when they looked up at her brilliance. According to author James Mooney, she said,

A Native American woman brings food to a dead relative's burial platform. Such offerings were thought to help the deceased on their journey to the afterlife.

"My grandchildren are ugly; they grin all over their faces when they look at me." But the Moon said, "I like my younger brothers [the people on earth]; I think they are very handsome"—because they always smiled pleasantly when they saw him in the sky at night, for his rays were milder.

The Sun was jealous and planned to kill all the people, so every day when she got near her daughter's house she sent down such sultry [hot] rays that there was a great fever and the people died by hundreds, until everyone had lost some friend and there was fear that no one would be left.[54]

Frightened by the now murderous Sun, the Cherokee people sought out the Little Men, a race of small, magical, forest-dwelling people, and asked them what to do. The Little Men informed the Cherokee that the Sun would have to be killed. One of the Little Men then changed a Cherokee warrior into a rattlesnake and commanded him to wait for the Sun at her daughter's doorway. When the Sun approached, the Rattlesnake was to bite her.

The Rattlesnake, however, was too eager. When the Sun's daughter opened her door in anticipation of the arrival of her mother, the Rattlesnake accidentally bit and killed her. When the Sun discovered her daughter's corpse, the plight of the Cherokee worsened. The Sun, devastated and sad, retreated into her daughter's house and refused to come out. As a result, humankind was plunged into perpetual darkness.

Again the Cherokee turned to the Little Men for a solution. This time the Little Men instructed the Cherokee to travel to the land of the dead to retrieve the deceased daughter of the Sun. The Little Men, says Mooney,

> told them [the Cherokee] that if they wanted the Sun to come out again they must bring her daughter back from Tsusgina'i, the Ghost country, in . . . the Darkening land in the west [the land of the dead]. They chose seven men to go, and gave each a sourwood rod a hand-breadth long. The Little Men told them that they must take a box with them, and when

Death and Nature

The natives of North America had great respect for the natural world on which they depended for sustenance, clothing, and shelter. Further, they believed that the death of a plant or an animal allowed for the survival of their tribes, and as a result, the Native Americans expressed gratitude to the natural world. This gratitude took many different forms. For example, in the Pacific Northwest, Native Americans celebrated a first-catch ceremony in which the first salmon of the year was placed on boughs of evergreen trees, a symbol of everlasting life, so that the tribe could thank the salmon for willingly sacrificing itself to sustain humankind. The salmon was then cooked, and each person of the tribe consumed a small piece of the sacred first fish. Afterward, the bones were returned to the water in the belief that the fish would live again. Likewise, on the eastern seaboard, Native Americans celebrated the Green Corn ceremony, an annual new year and purification ritual, in which they gave thanks to the corn they had harvested for its powers of sustaining human life. In these ways, Native Americans showed their appreciation for the death of the living things that sustained their own lives.

they got to Tsusgina'i they would find all the ghosts at a dance. They must stand outside the circle, and when the young woman [the Sun's daughter] passed in the dance they must strike her with the rods and she would fall to the ground. Then they must put her into the box and bring her back to her mother, but they must be very sure not to open the box, even a little way, until they were home again.[55]

The Ghost Country

As instructed by the Little Men, the seven Cherokee set out for the Darkening land with the rods and the box. They traveled for seven days. Finally, they arrived at the land of the dead in which the ghosts danced just as if they had been at home in a Cherokee settlement. The ghosts took no notice of the men even as they approached the daughter of the Sun, who danced in the outermost circle.

The Cherokee then set about following the instructions of the Little Men. According to Mooney's account of the legend:

As she [the daughter of the Sun] swung round to where the seven men were standing, one struck her with his rod and she turned her head and saw him. As she came around the second time another touched her with his rod, and then another and another, until at the seventh

round she fell out of the ring, and they put her in the box and closed the lid fast. The other ghosts seemed never to notice what had happened.[56]

Afterward, the men started back for the village. As they traveled, the girl began to come back to life and begged to be allowed out of the box. But the men made no answer and moved on. Later, the girl begged for something to eat, but they continued to ignore her pleas. Still later she asked for something to drink, but despite the desperation in her voice, the men continued toward home. When at last they were very near home, the girl again begged them to raise the lid just a little; she said she was smothering. By now, says Mooney, continuing the Cherokee story:

They were afraid she was really dying . . . so they lifted the lid a little to give her air, but as they did so there was a fluttering sound inside and something flew past them into the thicket and they heard a redbird cry, "kwish! kwish! kwish!" in the bushes. They shut down the lid and went on again to the settlements, but when they got there and opened the box it was empty. . . . If the men had kept the box closed, as the Little Men had told them to do, they would have brought her home safely, and we [humans] could bring back our other friends also from the Ghost country, but now when they die, we can never bring them back.[57]

Thus, while the Sun later agreed to continue to light the sky, humankind was destined to be forever separated from the world of the dead.

An Algonquian's Journey into the Afterlife

Not all tribal traditions held that humans could never be reunited with the dead, however. Some believed that people could journey to the afterlife to visit the

Native Americans believed that the afterlife was nearly identical to the land of the living.

deceased. One example is the Algonquian tale of the Island of the Blessed in which a young man is so overcome with grief over the death of his bride that he seeks the afterlife not to bring her back but to remain there with her. In the course of his adventures, however, the man learns of the value of life and therefore chooses not to hasten his own journey to the underworld.

Legend says that a young Algonquin man who learned that his fiancée had died on the morning they were to have been married was stricken with deep grief and sadness. Once one of the most spirited and courageous men of his tribe, after the death of his betrothed, the young man moped through the camp without engaging in any of his usual activities. His friends and family urged him to try to recover from his sadness, but instead, the young man became more depressed. Soon all he could do was spend his days and nights at the grave of the woman who was to have been his bride.

This vigil continued for many days until the young man overheard a conversation among tribal elders. According to author Lewis Spence,

> [The young man] was roused from his state of apathy one day . . . by hearing some old men discussing the existence of a path to the spirit world, which they supposed lay to the south. A gleam of hope shone in the young brave's breast,

and, worn with sorrow as he was, he armed himself and set off southward.

The young man's journey led him far away from the lands with which he was familiar, and [f]or a long time, he saw no appreciable change in his surroundings— rivers, mountains, lakes and forests similar to those of his own country environed him. But after a weary journey of many days he fancied he saw a difference. The sky was more blue, the prairie more fertile, the scenery more gloriously beautiful. From the conversation he had heard before he had set out, the young brave judged that he was nearing the spirit world.[58]

The Island of the Blessed

Eventually, the young man emerged from one of the forests to see a dwelling high up on a hill. Thinking that someone in the lodge might be able to direct him to the spirit world, the young man climbed the hill and announced his presence.

An aged man stepped into the doorway, and the young man relayed the story of his deceased fiancée and asked if the lodge dweller knew the location of the spirit world. The old man's response made the young man's heart leap. As Spence describes:

The Ghost Dance

One of the more interesting rites of the Native American peoples was called the Ghost Dance, a form of communication with a tribe's deceased ancestors developed in an effort to reject the influence of Europeans in North America and preserve tribal traditions. During the 1800s, as the U.S. government sought to push westward to expand the nation's borders, Native Americans suffered terrible losses: Their lands were seized; the buffalo they had depended on as food were killed; and the people themselves were victims of relocation programs, disease, war, and outright murder.

Taking various forms which depended on the tribe that adopted the practice, the Ghost Dance included a days-long marathon of special songs and dances meant to restore and encourage past traditions, including a solidarity between the living Native Americans and their deceased ancestors. In doing so, the tribes hoped to recreate the world of the Native Americans before the arrival of the Europeans.

Native Americans perform the Ghost Dance.

"Yes," said the old man gravely, throwing aside his cloak of swan's skin. "Only a few days ago she whom you seek rested in my lodge. If you will leave your body here you may follow her. To reach the Island of the Blessed [the spirit world] you must cross yonder gulf you see in the distance. But I warn you the crossing will be no easy matter. Do you still wish to go?"

"Oh, yes, yes," cried the warrior eagerly, and as the words were uttered he felt himself suddenly grow lighter. The whole aspect, too, of the scene was changed. Everything looked brighter and more ethereal [heavenly]. He found himself in a moment walking through thickets which offered no resistance to his passage, and he knew that he was a spirit, traveling in the spirit world.[59]

Traveling in this manner, the young man made his way to the wide gulf. Fortunately he discovered a canoe upon the shore. The canoe was cut from a single white stone, and it sparkled in the sunlight. The young man lost no time in guiding the canoe into the water.

Even more surprising than the presence of the canoe was what the young man saw as he dipped the oar into the water for the first time. Parallel to his canoe was a second canoe carrying his dead fiancée. She imitated all his movements; in this way, the betrothed couple headed side by side toward the spirit world, the Island of the Blessed. But the easy rowing conditions that marked the beginning of the trip were not to last. As Spence describes:

> When they were about halfway across [the gulf] a sudden storm arose, and the huge waves threatened to engulf them. Many other people had embarked upon the perilous waters by this time, some of whom perished in the furious tempest [storm]. But the youth and maiden still battled on bravely, never losing sight of one another. . . . And after a weary struggle they felt their canoes grate on the shore.

The couple lived in happiness together for some time on the Island of the Blessed. They enjoyed the plenty of the land, missing none of the benefits of the life they would have had on earth if the girl had lived. However, one day, while walking on the island with his betrothed, the young man heard the Master of Life, the creator of humankind, whispering in his ear. Spence concludes the legend thus: [The Master of Life said,] "You must finish your mortal course. . . . You will become a great chief among your own people. Rule wisely and well, and when your earthly career is over you shall return to your bride."[60]

Thus, the young man understood that he would have to leave.

Sadly, the young man said goodbye to the girl. He went back to the white stone canoe and took his leave of the island. He traveled back to the lodge of the old man, where his spirit returned to his body. And, after giving his thanks to the old man, the young man made his way once again to his village.

Although he had to leave the Island of the Blessed, he was no longer without hope, for he knew that he would see the girl he loved again when he died. Secure in that knowledge, he became a gentle and wise ruler for many years before he passed on to the Island of the Blessed. As in the stories of other tribes, the existence of an afterlife helped a bereaved young man come to terms with the death of a loved one. Further, his trip to the afterlife illustrated the Algonquian's view of the afterlife; the Island of the Blessed was an idealized version of the life the Algonquian knew on earth.

Tribe members gather under the funeral scaffold of their chief. Some Native Americans believed that the living could visit the dead in the afterlife.

The Algonquian tale shares many similarities with the legends of the Pawnee and Cherokee. These Native American people believed that the spirits of the dead are accessible to the living and that the dead have the same pleasures and duties they had during life. Thus, despite the myriad tribes whose legends compose the Native American mythological tradition, certain basic concepts with respect to death and the afterlife are present in almost all tribal belief systems.

Myths of Tribal Africa: Rich and Varied

Chapter Six

African mythology, one of the oldest and richest mythic heritages in the world, permeates many varied cultures and is expressed in hundreds of languages. A detailed overview of all these legends would cover many volumes. Despite the innumerable cultural and linguistic differences found in any study of Africa, however, traditional beliefs about death and the afterlife display a surprising number of similarities.

African Conceptions of Death

Notably, in most African cultures, humans were thought to have been created to live forever in a perfect world, where a benign creator provided for all their wants. Death was often seen as the result of a last-minute change of plans by the creator, or as punishment for an error committed by early earth-dwellers; other stories existed as well.

Whatever its origin, death was often characterized as an actual being or creature. In *Introduction to African Religion*, author John S. Mbiti elaborates:

> [African] people try to visualize death in personal terms. Some think of it as a monster, others as an animal, and many regard it as a kind of spirit. It is said in Uganda, for example, that the spirit of death never laughs. And who can blame it, since its work is to kill, destroy, take away, and terrorize people everywhere.[61]

No matter how death was depicted, however, it was always permanent. Although a living person might accidentally stray into the underworld and be

Young men in the Lafit Mountains of Africa play pipes at a warrior's funeral.

allowed to escape, once death had occurred, there was no coming back. Thus despite the number of legends about the origin and nature of death, Mbiti says, "there are no myths in Africa about how death might one day be overcome or removed from the world. . . . Death spoilt the original paradise of men."[62]

Escape from the Underworld

The deceased themselves could not leave death behind, but a mortal who stumbled upon it could escape. Myths recounting such adventures emphasize the eventual reality of death as well as

the ability of the living to struggle against it. Indeed, many African tales discuss the escape of mortals from the underworld. One example is the Zulu legend of Uncama, a farmer who accidentally crosses into the underworld only to retrace his steps and return to the land of the living. Another recurrent story is that of a heroic journey in which a person, who for some reason finds himself in the underworld, must defeat death to return to his home on earth. Such is the case in the Angolan tale of the hero brothers Sudika-mbambi and Kabundungulu in which the younger of the brothers must rescue the older from the underworld.

The Lizard and the Chameleon

The Zulu tribes comprise Bantu-speaking people who live primarily in southern Africa. Their traditional belief in death is rooted in the idea that mortality was the result of a last minute decision by the creator, called Unkulunkulu, meaning "the Very Old."

According to the Zulu legend, Unkulunkulu was undecided as to whether humankind should be granted immortality or whether people should die. After some thought, Unkulunkulu decided that he would in fact allow humans to live forever. To communicate his decision, Unkulunkulu summoned one of his servants, a chameleon, and instructed him to travel to humankind and to tell the people they would not have to die.

The chameleon started off, but he moved very slowly. On the way, he stopped to eat the fruit of a mulberry tree, and periodically he fell asleep in the warmth of the sun. Meanwhile, Unkulunkulu changed his mind and instead decided that men should know death. He called another servant, this time a lizard, and commanded him to run to humankind with the message that they would die.

The lizard set out immediately, running hard and fast. He soon passed the slow chameleon and reached humankind first.

Zulu warriors pose for a photographer. The Zulu of southern Africa believe that all humans eventually must face death.

The lizard then immediately informed the humans of Unkulunkulu's decision: Humans would die. Soon after the lizard had gone back to his master, the chameleon appeared with the exact opposite message. But it was too late. From then on, according to the Zulu, all humans had to face death.

The Moon and the Insect

Likewise the Khoi of southwest Africa also believed that death was an inescapable force that had been arbitrarily forced on humankind. Yet unlike the Zulu, the Khoi believed that humans were created by the Moon and that death was the result of a mistake on the part of the Moon's messenger.

According to Khoi tradition, just after the creation of humankind, the Moon commanded an Insect to crawl to men and inform them that they would have eternal lives corresponding to the phases of the moon. As the moon changed shape from full moon to half moon to new moon and back, so too would humans be born, grow old, die and be reborn. Death, then would not be the end of humankind, but only a recurring phase. As Clyde W. Ford relates, "The Moon [said to the Insect]: 'Go to men and tell them, "As I die, and dying live; so you [humans] shall also die, and dying live."'"[63]

Following the Moon's instructions, the Insect started off on his journey, crawling slowly over the earth on his way to humankind. But the Insect was overtaken by the Hare, a familiar figure in the mythology of the region. The Hare was curious about the Insect's errand, and the Insect told the Hare of the Moon's command.

The Hare, noting that the Insect was not the swiftest messenger among the Moon's servants, asked the Insect if he could be the one to inform humans of the Moon's decision. The Insect agreed to this change in plans. The Hare, however, confused the Moon's message and accidentally delivered the wrong one. As Ford writes:

[The Hare] ran off, and when he reached men, he said, "As I die and dying perish, in the same manner you shall also die and come wholly to an end."

The Hare then returned to the Moon and told her what he had said to men. The Moon reproached him angrily, saying, "Do you dare tell the people a thing that I have not said?"[64]

Angry, the Moon scooped up a piece of wood and struck the Hare on the nose with it. The Khoi believe that is why the nose of the Hare is slit. Further, the Khoi contend, humans continued to believe what the Hare mistakenly told them, and for this reason they are doomed to die.

God and Death

The Congolese of the shores of Lake Kivu in present-day Zaire had a decidedly different idea. They felt that death was the result of an error committed by humans. Indeed, contend the Congolese, not only was death allowed to lay waste to the once immortal and protected humans, but the arrival of death also signified the beginning of humanity's distant relationship with God.

According to Congolese legend, God, after creating humanity, told people that they would never die. As a result, the world became more and more populated until Death, an immortal being, became upset that the human population was growing so steadily. Yet Death could not interfere with the affairs of humans because God was always on the watch; if Death did try to interfere, God would attack him, forcing him to retreat to his underground residence.

One day, though, God grew careless. Having business in heaven, God stopped watching humanity for a short time. Death took advantage of this opportunity by seizing his first victim, an old woman. When the people of the earth learned that the old woman was no longer living, they grieved, for she was the first person ever to die. Afterward, they dug a grave and buried her.

However, because the dead woman was the first to die, her spirit did not know that it was necessary to leave the body it had been inhabiting. Thus it made every effort

This engraving shows a Congolese king. Congolese legend says that Death claims lives to keep the population from becoming too dense.

to revive the corpse. As is stated in the *New Larousse Encyclopedia of Mythology:*

Some days later the earth on the grave began to rise as if the dead person was returning to life. The dead person was an old woman, who had left several children and daughters-in-law. She was about to rise from the dead, when one of her daughters-in-law noticed it. She ran off for boiling water which she poured on her mother-in-law's grave. Then, making a pestle [a tool used to pound grain into meal] she kept beating the ground saying: "Die! What is dead should stay dead!"[65]

The next day, the earth around the grave of the old woman began to rise again. Once more, the daughter-in-law poured boiling water on the grave and beat it with the pestle, while shouting that what is dead should stay dead. This time the spirit of the old woman accepted the message and stopped trying to restore the dead person to the world of the living.

Shortly thereafter, God returned to the earth and noticed immediately the absence of the old woman. When he was told by the others what had happened, God decided to pursue Death and demand that there be no more victims. Ordering all humanity to remain in their homes, God proceeded to scour the earth in search of Death.

After many days, God located Death, and a chase ensued. While fleeing, Death noticed an old woman who had foolishly left her home in favor of hiding in the bushes. Death asked the woman to hide him and promised a reward for her assistance. Enticed by Death's promise, the old woman lifted to her armpits the skin that enclosed her body, and Death slipped beneath it and into her belly.

When God arrived he perceived the old woman's foolishness and was furious. As the *New Larousse* describes:

God . . . threw himself on [the old woman] saying: . . . "The best thing is to kill her, take Death out, and then kill it." God had barely finished killing the old woman, when a young woman came out of her hut. . . . Death instantly fled from the old woman's body and hid in the young woman's. Seeing this God said: "Well! Since they [people] keep thwarting my efforts, let them take the consequences and die!"[66]

From then on, God chose to watch humanity only from heaven, refusing to live on earth. Death then was free to leave his underground kingdom to claim other lives whenever he saw fit.

Uncama Goes to Mosima

Whether a mistake on the part of the creator or a punishment for humanity's disobedience, death was terrifying to the Africans. Consequently, many African traditions also discuss the underworld in terms of fear and the need to try to escape. The Zulu tale of Uncama's journey to Mosima, which means "the abyss," involves the accidental discovery of the underworld by a mortal lucky enough to be able to effect an escape.

The story begins with Uncama's failed efforts to grow the local grain called millet. Although the millet grew well at first, every time it ripened, a porcupine ravaged the garden and devoured the entire crop.

Unnatural Causes of Death

The belief persists in most African tribes that most human deaths attributed by modern medicine to old age instead resulted from unnatural forces: sorcery, malevolent spirits, or curses. As scholar John S. Mbiti explains in *Introduction to African Religion:*

People [in Africa] believe that sorcery, witchcraft, and evil magic cause death. Therefore, when someone has died, people often try to find out who has used sorcery . . . against the dead person. Someone is often blamed for it, and in some cases the suspect may be beaten to death, fined or thrown out of the district. . . .

If the blame is not laid on the use of sorcery . . . spirits may be blamed. These might be spirits of people who have had a grudge against the person, or whose bodies were not properly buried, or who have been neglected by their relatives for some reason or another. . . .

Curses, broken taboos or oaths are sometimes believed to cause deaths. Therefore they are feared, and people endeavor to avoid being cursed or breaking oaths.

This went on for a very long time until Uncama finally decided to follow the porcupine and kill it. As Ford writes:

At length [Uncama] waited for a day on which there was an abundance of dew [so he could see traces of the porcupine's passage]. On that day he arose and said, "Today then I can follow [the porcupine] . . . if it has eaten of the garden, for where it has gone the dew will be brushed off. At length I may discover where it has gone into its hole." . . . So Uncama, with weapons in hand, embarked upon the marauding porcupine's trail of dew, and upon discovering its hole, he pressed ahead, down into the depths, without further hesitation, saying, "I will go till I reach it, and kill it."[67]

Uncama descended into the hole, yet, to his surprise, he discovered that the porcupine's hole led to Mosima, the underworld. Uncama had inadvertently stumbled onto a path that led to the land of the dead.

In Mosima, he saw villages and people going about the same routines they had practiced in the land of the living. Although the people he encountered were not overtly threatening, Uncama worried that they would want to keep him there, to kill him in order to trap him in the underworld. As author Ford describes:

> "Ho! What place is this?" [Uncama] said. "I am following a porcupine, yet I have come upon a dwelling."

At this point Uncama became fearful and he began to retreat, walking backward along the path he had thus far traversed, anxiously pondering his fate with the thought: "Let me not go to these people, for I do not know them; perhaps they will kill me."[68]

When he was once again in the world of the living, Uncama made his way back to his village only to discover that his wife and neighbors believed him to be dead; he had been absent much longer than he had realized. His wife had already burned all his clothes and possessions and was making preparations to return to her family, as was the custom of their tribe in the event of a husband's death.

After celebrating Uncama's return, the neighbors asked him where he had been for so long. Uncama related the astonishing details of his disappearance to his people:

> "I have come from a great distance—from those who live underground. I followed a porcupine; I came to a village and heard dogs

Young Zulu in traditional dress sit and talk. The Zulu culture tells a story of Uncama, a mortal who was lucky enough to escape from the underworld.

baying, children crying; I saw people moving around; the smoke from their cooking fires was rising. So I came back. I was afraid, I thought they would kill me. And it is because I feared and returned that you see me this day."[69]

Uncama's tale illustrates both the accessibility of the underworld, and the frightening aspects that make it a place mortals would not want to visit. Only through his aversion to the world of the dead was Uncama able to preserve his life.

Descent to the Spirit World

Other traditions hold that the prospect of escaping death involves much more heroic ambition. The myths of the Ambundu people of Angola contend that only their greatest mythical heroes returned from the underworld and then only after successfully challenging Kalunga-ngombe, the king of death himself. The story of the hero brothers Sudika-mbambi and Kabundungulu is a tale of one such journey and return. It also becomes a reminder for the Ambundu that life after death awaits them in the afterworld.

Sudika-mbambi was one of the greatest of Angolan heroes. He was born both standing and speaking, and he carried his weaponry from his mother's womb. His younger brother, Kabundungulu, also was born fully armed.

The story of Sudika-mbambi's journey to the underworld began when he left the family under his younger brother's protection and departed to confront the Makishi, the enemies of his family. While alone on a trail, Sudika-mbambi made the acquaintance of four supernatural beings called the Kipalendes, each of whom boasted of unique magical powers. To prove their claims, the Kipalendes agreed to join Sudika-mbambi in his fight against the Makishi.

On the first day of fighting, three of the Kipalendes fought at Sudika-mbambi's side while the fourth guarded their camp. The lone Kipalende was approached by an elderly lady who promised him that if he could defeat her, he could marry her granddaughter. Thinking the task to be a simple one, the Kipalende accepted. The old woman, however, trounced him severely. The following day, a different Kipalende remained behind to confront the old lady, but he too was defeated. For two more days this continued, and then it was Sudika-mbambi's turn.

Sudika-mbambi defeated and killed the old lady, thereby earning her granddaughter as his wife, but the Kipalendes were chagrined because they had been outdone by a mortal youth. Thus they decided to kill him and take the old lady's granddaughter for their own. As Ford relates:

> The Kipalendes were actually jealous of Sudika-mbambi. "A mere child has bested us," they complained. "We must kill him, but how?" They plotted Sudika-mbambi's death by digging a hole

African Funeral Practices

Although each African tribe possessed its own rituals connected with the process of burying the dead, some key elements are consistent throughout much of tribal Africa. In many parts of Africa, for instance, it was customary to bury a deceased person's belongings with his or her body; such belongings might have included spears, bows and arrows, furniture, food, ornaments, or tools. In addition, once the body was buried, the tribe members typically performed a ceremony over the grave; the type of ceremony, though, could vary greatly. If the person were of minor standing in the tribe, the ceremony often was sparsely attended. In other situations, when a person of great wealth or social standing died, the ceremony was a much more complicated affair, and the proceedings were also used as a forum for selecting and installing the rightful familial heir.

In nearly all cases, after the burial ceremony, food was served to the attendees. This served two purposes. It meant that the funeral guests would stay and provide company for those most affected by the death, primarily the family; and it was also a way to thank all those who had come to the funeral. At the feast, songs of mourning were typically sung. In some tribes, immediate family members shaved off their hair; in other locations, survivors smeared themselves with white clay or refrained from normal daily activities—including washing, or milking animals—for a set number of days. Regardless of the act, the aim of the sacrifice was the same: To show respect for the dead by engaging in a unique ritual to demonstrate that someone important to the family had passed on.

People gather to watch dancers perform at a funeral ceremony.

Angolan tribesmen perform a traditional dance. Some Angolans believe that only their greatest mythical heroes return from the underworld.

in the ground and covering it with a mat spread on top. "Come, Sudika-mbambi, have a seat here," they said. When Sudika-mbambi sat down he dropped into the hole and the Kipalendes quickly covered the hole with dirt. They took the young woman [the old woman's granddaughter] for their own.[70]

Although the Kipalendes succeeded in tricking Sudika-mbambi, they had underestimated his heroic skills. Sudika-mbambi managed to enter the world of the dead while still alive. According to Ford:

At the bottom of the hole, a road leading to Kalunga-ngombe, the [Lord of the Dead], opened up for Sudika-mbambi. Along the road, he happened on an old woman who was hoeing. . . . Sudika-mbambi greeted her, then asked if she would show him the road from there.

"Two paths lead from here," she uttered, "a wide path and a narrow path. Take to the narrow path; do not take the wide path or you will go astray. And when you finally arrive outside Kalunga-ngombe's, you must carry a jug of red pepper and a jug of wisdom."[71]

The old woman produced jars containing the appropriate contents and gave them to Sudika-mbambi. He thanked her for her assistance and followed her advice; in this way, Sudika-mbambi was well prepared for his errand in the heart of the underworld.

Death of a Hero

On Sudika-mbambi's arrival in the underworld, Kalunga-ngombe appeared to him and asked his business. In a challenge meant to prove his strength as a warrior and hopefully secure his escape from the underworld, Sudika-mbambi responded by saying that he had come to marry the lord's daughter.

Surprised by this, the Lord of the Dead decided to test Sudika-mbambi to determine his worth as a potential son-in-law. As Ford relates:

"Well," said the Lord of [the Dead], "you shall marry my daughter, but only if you possess a jug of red pepper and a jug of wisdom."

When Sudika-mbambi produced the required items, Kalunga-ngombe covered his surprise with laughter. . . . But the next morning, he backed off, saying, "If you want my daughter, then first you will have to rescue her

from the great serpent, Kinioka kia Tumba!"[72]

Sudika-mbambi agreed to this challenge. He confronted the two-headed serpent where it guarded the daughter of the Lord of the Dead, chopped off both its heads, and returned to Kalunga-ngombe with the girl in tow. Yet, the Lord of the Dead was still not satisfied, as he was reluctant to give up his daughter. He wanted to test Sudika-mbambi with another challenge; this one would prove to be the young man's undoing. As Ford describes:

Kalunga-ngombe . . . challenged [Sudika-mbambi] to kill Kimbiji kia Malenda, the crocodile, master of the underworld abyss. Sudika-mbambi fished for Kimbiji with a suckling pig as bait, but the crocodile was too strong for him and pulled Sudika-mbambi into the water where he was swallowed whole.[73]

Resurrection

The hero Sudika-mbambi would have been trapped in the belly of the crocodile for all eternity had it not been for the efforts of his younger brother. For, when Sudika-mbambi failed to return home, Kabundungulu assumed that something had gone wrong. He followed the trail of his brother until he came upon the four Kipalendes. When the Kipalendes refused to divulge the whereabouts of his brother, Kabundungulu

Ghosts of the Dead

The belief in ghosts was consistent throughout tribal Africa. Indeed, many tribes believed that the process of dying involved first becoming a ghost that haunted the land of the living until the proper ceremonies were performed to release it into the afterlife.

The process by which the soul vacated the body was intricately connected to a person's breath because breath and soul were thought to be closely related. In fact, many African tribes believed that the breath was actually a piece of the soul. Thus, upon death, one stopped breathing because the soul had departed from the body via the mouth or nose, or through the eyes.

Once the soul had left the body, however, it did not necessarily let go of the living world. Instead, many tribes believed that the soul would stay near the body, perhaps not even realizing that the body was dead, until the tribe had conducted the funeral rites necessary to convey to the soul that it should disappear into the afterlife. It was believed that if these funerary rites were not performed, the soul would haunt the living. African tribes therefore placed a huge importance on the proper burial of a loved one both for the sake of the dead and for the peace of mind of the living.

surmised that they had tried to kill him. Kabundungulu then threatened to kill the Kipalendes if they did not reveal the location of Sudka-mbambi's body. The Kipalendes relented.

Using the pit that had trapped his brother as an entrance, Kabundungulu began his descent to the underworld to locate and save Sudika-mbambi. According to Ford:

> Kabundungulu . . . struck out on the road his brother had taken to the realm of Kalunga-ngombe. He met the old woman, who showed him the way to Kalunga-ngombe's abode, and there he

demanded of the Lord of Death to know his brother's condition.

Kalunga-ngombe informed the younger hero that his elder brother had been swallowed by Kimbiji. So Kabundungulu fished the monstrous crocodile out of the water with a pig as bait, took his knife, and cut Kimbiji open. There he found the bones of Sudika-mbambi, which he gathered together, uttering, "My elder brother, arise!"

Sudika-mbambi was thus resurrected, and to him Kalunga-ngombe finally gave his daughter.[74]

Homecoming

The brothers returned home with both the daughter of the Lord of the Dead and the old lady's granddaughter whom the Kipalendes had hoped to steal from Sudika-mbambi. The women, though, would prove to destroy the love the brothers had for each other. For even though Kabundungulu had rescued his older brother, Sudika-mbambi was unwilling to let him marry either woman. As Ford relates:

African tribesmen beat drums to mourn the death of a warrior.

Finally arriving home, the younger brother said, "My elder brother, give me one wife, for you have two, and I have none."

But Sudika-mbambi took offense at such a suggestion and told his younger brother never to mention it to him again. . . . The two began to quarrel, striking each other with the intentions to kill, but neither one's powers were stronger than the other's. Finally they grew weary of fighting and agreed to part ways— the elder brother, Sudika-mbambi, heading east; his younger brother, Kabundungulu, traveling west.[75]

The Ambundu believed that the sound of thunder in the east was the still-angry voice of Sudika-mbambi, and its echoed response in the west was the cry of Kabundungulu.

The sound of thunder was a two-fold reminder for the people of Angola. It reminded them that death was something humans had to face and of the afterlife itself. Just as the two brothers were able to defeat death, becoming the sound of thunder as a result, the Ambundu believed that they had to struggle in life against the powers of death so that when they did die, they, like the hero brothers, would live on in the afterlife.

Regardless of the tradition, African mythology tries to explain both the reason for the advent of death and also the appearance of the underworld, a place from which only a few have managed to escape. Ultimately, the defeat of death by the few heroes who returned from the underworld in turn helps explain to those who are still living that there is indeed an afterlife. Thus, although the living must die, they are assured of another life beyond this one by the testimonies of those few individuals who have both visited the underworld and returned to the land of the living.

Notes

Introduction: The Meaning of Death

1. Alan E. Bernstein, *The Formation of Hell*. Ithaca, NY: Cornell University Press, 1993, p. ix.

Chapter 1: Ancient Egypt: Truth and Judgment

2. Siegfried Morenz, *Egyptian Religion*, trans. Ann E. Keep. Ithaca, NY: Cornell University Press, 1973, p. 113.
3. Quoted in A. Rosalie David, *The Ancient Egyptians: Religious Beliefs and Practices*. London: Routledge and Kegan Paul, 1982, pp. 201–203.
4. Bernstein, *The Formation of Hell*, p. 12.
5. Alan Shorter, *The Egyptian Gods*. San Bernardino, CA: The Borgo, 1994, p. 54.
6. Quoted in Shorter, *The Egyptian Gods*, p. 54.
7. Shorter, *The Egyptian Gods*, p. 54.
8. Quoted in Shorter, *The Egyptian Gods*, p. 55.
9. Quoted in Shorter, *The Egyptian Gods*, p. 54.
10. Quoted in Shorter, *The Egyptian Gods*, p. 54.
11. Shorter, *The Egyptian Gods*, p. 85.
12. Shorter, *The Egyptian Gods*, p. 88.

Chapter 2: Ancient Greece: Mortal Death and Immortal Imprisonment

13. Robert Garland, *The Greek Way of Death*. Ithaca, NY: Cornell University Press, 1985, p. 51.
14. Quoted in Garland, *The Greek Way of Death*, p. 51.
15. Apollodorus, in *The Library of Greek Mythology*, trans. Robin Hard. Oxford: Oxford University Press, 1997, p. 28.
16. Homer, "The Hymn to Demeter," in *The Homeric Hymns*, trans. Charles Boer. Dallas, TX: Spring Publications, 1970, pp. 122–23.
17. Homer, *The Odyssey*, trans. Robert Fitzgerald. Garden City, NY: Anchor Books, 1963, p. 445.
18. *Bulfinch's Mythology*. New York: Crowell, 1962, p. 267.
19. Apollodorus, in *The Library of Greek Mythology*, p. 83.
20. *Bulfinch's Mythology*, p. 186.
21. *Bulfinch's Mythology*, pp. 186–87.
22. Homer, *The Odyssey*, p. 192.
23. Homer, *The Odyssey*, p. 198.
24. Homer, *The Odyssey*, p. 202.

Chapter 3: The Celts: The Fairiefolk of the Afterlife

25. Proinsias MacCana, *Celtic Mythology*. London: Hamlyn, 1970, pp. 123–24.
26. Lady Gregory, *Cuchulain of Muirthemne*: Chapter XX. www.belinus.co.uk/folklore/FaerypiecesGregory2.htm. December 20, 2000.
27. Lady Gregory, *Cuchulain of Muirthemne*.
28. Lady Gregory, *Cuchulain of Muirthemne*.
29. *The Voyage of Bran*, www.as.wvu.edu/eng101/www/clc/vob/bran.html.
30. *The Voyage of Bran*.
31. *The Voyage of Bran*.
32. *Bulfinch's Mythology*, p. 519.
33. *Bulfinch's Mythology*, p. 520.
34. *Bulfinch's Mythology*, p. 520.

Chapter 4: Aztecs: Death, Sacrifice, and Creation

35. Quoted in Miguel León-Portilla, "Those Made Worthy by Divine Sacrifice: The Faith of Ancient Mexico," in Gary H. Gossen, ed., *South and Meso-American Native Spirituality*. New York: Crossroad, p. 41.
36. León-Portilla, "Those Made Worthy by Diving Sacrifice," p. 44.
37. Quoted in Karl Taube, *Aztec and Maya Myths*. London and Austin: British Museum Press and University of Texas Press, 1993, p. 37.
38. Taube, *Aztec and Maya Myths*, p. 38.
39. Quoted in Taube, *Aztec and Maya Myths*, p. 38.
40. Taube, *Aztec and Maya Myths*, p. 39.
41. Taube, *Aztec and Maya Myths*, p. 39.
42. Taube, *Aztec and Maya Myths*, p. 41.
43. Taube, *Aztec and Maya Myths*, p. 41.
44. Quoted in Taube, *Aztec and Maya Myths*, p. 41.
45. Taube, *Aztec and Maya Myths*, p. 42.
46. Quoted in Taube, *Aztec and Maya Myths*, p. 42.
47. Quoted in Taube, *Aztec and Maya Myths*, p. 42.
48. Taube, *Aztec and Maya Myths*, p. 44.
49. León-Portilla, "Those Made Worthy by Divine Sacrifice," pp. 43–44.

Chapter 5: Natives of North America: In Death as in Life

50. James L. Haley, *Apaches: A History and Cultural Portrait*. Garden City, NY: Doubleday, 1981, p. 177.
51. George Bird Grinnell, *Pawnee, Blackfoot and Cheyenne*, ed. Dee Brown. New York: Charles Scribner's Sons, 1961, p. 78.
52. Grinnell, *Pawnee, Blackfoot and Cheyenne*, p. 79.
53. Grinnell, *Pawnee, Blackfoot and Cheyenne*, p. 79.
54. James Mooney, *Myths of the Cherokee and Sacred Formulas of the Cherokee*. Nashville, TN: Charles and Randy Elder, 1982, p. 252.
55. Mooney, *Myths of the Cherokee and Sacred Formulas of the Cherokee*, p. 253.
56. Mooney, *Myths of the Cherokee and Sacred Formulas of the Cherokee*, p. 253.
57. Mooney, *Myths of the Cherokee and Sacred Formulas of the Cherokee*, p. 254.
58. Lewis Spence, *Myths and Legends of the North American Indians*. London: George C. Harrap, 1914, p. 162.
59. Spence, *Myths and Legends of the North American Indians*, p. 163.
60. Spence, *Myths and Legends of the North American Indians*, p. 164.

Chapter 6: Myths of Tribal Africa: Rich and Varied

61. John S. Mbiti, *Introduction to African Religion*. Oxford: Heinemann, 1975, p. 117.
62. Mbiti, *Introduction to African Religion*, p. 117.
63. Clyde W. Ford, *The Hero with an African Face: Mythic Wisdom of Traditional Africa*. New York: Bantam, 1999, p. 193.
64. Ford, *The Hero with an African Face*, p. 193.
65. Felix Guirand, *New Larousse Encyclopedia of Mythology*. London: Hamlyn, 1976, p. 482.

66. Guirand, *New Larousse Encyclopedia of Mythology*, p. 483.

67. Ford, *The Hero with an African Face*, p. 19.

68. Ford, *The Hero with an African Face*, p. 20.

69. Ford, *The Hero with an African Face*, p. 20.

70. Ford, *The Hero with an African Face*, p. 40.

71. Ford, *The Hero with an African Face*, p. 40.

72. Ford, *The Hero with an African Face*, p. 42.

73. Ford, *The Hero with an African Face*, p. 43.

74. Ford, *The Hero with an African Face*, p. 44.

75. Ford, *The Hero with an African Face*, p. 44.

For Further Reading

Roger D. Abrahams, *African Folktales: Traditional Stories of the Black World*. New York: Pantheon, 1983. This book features a collection of ninety-five traditional African tales, including many about the beliefs concerning the dead, all of which are based on some of the earliest known written records of the original oral tales.

Richard Erdoes, ed., *American Indian Myths and Legends*. New York: Pantheon, 1984. This book offers a highly diverse selection of over a hundred American Indian tales, including some that involve ghosts and/or the spirit world.

Edith Hamilton, *Mythology*. Boston: Little, Brown, 1942. Renowned mythologian Edith Hamilton's classic collection of the most important of Greek and Roman myths and legends provides an excellent introduction into the realm of classical mythology.

Geraldine Harris, *Gods and Pharaohs from Egyptian Mythology*. New York: Peter Bedrick Books, 1993. A collection of the key myths within Egyptian mythology; includes well-told accounts of the Egyptian afterlife. The author has a reader-friendly approach that makes the material very accessible.

Works Consulted

Books

Apollodorus, in *The Library of Greek Mythology*. Trans. Robin Hard. Oxford: Oxford University Press, 1997. The definitive translation of one the first complete collections of the legends and myths of ancient Greece.

Alan E. Bernstein, *The Formation of Hell*. Ithaca, NY: Cornell University Press, 1993. The author looks at the development of modern visions of hell from a historical, multireligious perspective.

Bulfinch's Mythology. New York: Crowell, 1962. A relatively recent edition of the complete collection of ancient mythologies by nineteenth-century mythologian Thomas Bulfinch, one of the most renowned specialists of modern times.

Duane Champagne, ed., *The Native North American Almanac*. Detroit: Gale Research, 1994. A reference guide that explores the customs, practices, and beliefs of the present-day Native Americans of the United States and Canada.

A. Rosalie David, *The Ancient Egyptians: Religious Beliefs and Practices*. London: Routledge and Kegan Paul, 1982. David's book offers a chronologically ordered survey of Egyptian religious beliefs.

Clyde W. Ford, *The Hero with an African Face: Mythic Wisdom of Traditional Africa*. New York: Bantam, 1999. The author combines discussions of African myth and religion with modern interpretations for a contemporary audience. A study in the influence and value of the African myth.

Henri Frankfort, *Ancient Egyptian Religion*. New York: Harper & Row, 1961. A very detailed look at the socioreligious implications on numerous facets of life for the ancient Egyptians, including social structures.

Robert Garland, *The Greek Way of Death*. Ithaca, NY: Cornell University Press, 1985. An in-depth sociological look at the treatment of death in ancient Greece.

Sam D. Gill and Irene F. Sullivan, *A Dictionary of Native American Mythology*. Santa Barbara, CA: ABC-CLIO, 1992. A terse reference guide, ideal for cross-referencing different tribal traditions based on theme or mythic idea.

Miranda Green, *Celtic Myths (The Legendary Past)*. Austin: University of Texas Press, 1994. Green uses the works of contemporary commentators from the Classical world, later Christian scribes recording oral traditions, and archaeological evidence to discuss Celtic myths and their religious beliefs and rituals.

———, *The Gods of the Celts*. Totowa, New Jersey: Barnes & Noble, 1986. An overview of Celtic religion from about 500 B.C. to A.D. 400 that examines the gods, rituals, cults, sacred places, symbolism, and imagery of the Celtic peoples.

George Bird Grinnell, *Pawnee, Blackfoot and Cheyenne*. Ed. Dee Brown. New York: Charles Scribner's Sons, 1961. Written in the nineteenth century by the founder of the Audubon Society, the explorer George Bird Grinnell, this compilation of personal studies of the author's three favorite tribes includes in-depth looks at the folklore and customs of the Plains Indians in the late–nineteenth century.

Felix Guirand, *New Larousse Encyclopedia of Mythology*. London: Hamlyn, 1976. A general overview of the mythologies of the world, with a general introduction by the well-known scholar of mythology, Robert Graves.

James L. Haley, *Apaches: A History and Cultural Portrait*. Garden City, NY: Doubleday, 1981. An in-depth account of the Apache as a people, including their customs and religion, along with a discussion of the reasons for and effects of the near-decimation of Apache culture by the United States.

Homer, *The Iliad*. Trans. Robert Fagles. New York: Viking, 1990. A recent definitive verse translation of the events of the Trojan War.

———, *The Odyssey*. Trans. Robert Fitzgerald. Garden City, NY: Anchor Books, 1963. A translation of the classic original tale of Odysseus's ten-year journey to his home in Ithaca at the end of the Trojan War.

The Homeric Hymns. Trans. Charles Boer. Dallas: Spring Publications, 1970. The definitive collection of the ancient Greek hymns initially attributed to Homer.

Frederick E. Hoxie, ed., *Encyclopedia of North American Indians*. Boston: Houghton Mifflin, 1996. A strong overview of the beliefs, history, and culture of the natives of North America.

Miguel León-Portilla, *The Aztec Image of Self and Society*. Salt Lake City: University of Utah Press, 1992. A comprehensive sociological, ethnological, and archaeological survey of the Aztec people and psychology.

———, "Those Made Worthy by Divine Sacrifice: The Faith of Ancient Mexico," in Gary H. Gossen ed., *South and Meso-American Native Spirituality*. New York: Crossroad, 1993. A detailed look at the motivations—religious, lifestyle, and otherwise—that contributed to the Aztec belief in the necessity of sacrifice.

Proinsias MacCana, *Celtic Mythology*. London: Hamlyn, 1970. A thorough look at Celtic mythology through the study of surviving texts and archaeological data. Includes a comprehensive selection of detailed photographs of archaeological discoveries.

John S. Mbiti, *Introduction to African Religion*. Oxford: Heinemann, 1975. A strong general introduction to the religious beliefs and practices of the African continent.

James Mooney, *Myths of the Cherokee and Sacred Formulas of the Cherokee*. Nashville, TN: Charles and Randy Elder, 1982. A collection of the myths and beliefs of the Cherokee based on the one of the original annual reports for the U.S. government.

Siegfried Morenz, *Egyptian Religion*. Trans. Ann E. Keep. Ithaca, NY: Cornell University Press, 1973. An authoritative look at the rites and practices of the ancient Egyptians with numerous references to original manuscripts and other sources. The author's aim is to expose the complex ideas and ethos behind the myths themselves.

Ovid (Publius Ovidius Naso), *Metamorphoses*. Trans. Mary M. Innes. Harmonds-Worth: Penguin Classics, 1955. The definitive translation from the Latin, of one of the most famous storytellers of all time.

Alan Shorter, *The Egyptian Gods*. San Bernardino, CA: The Borgo, 1994. A practiced and thorough look into the myths of the ancient Egyptians, including the meaning of these myths within what can be known regarding the cultural context of the ancient Egyptians themselves.

Lewis Spence, *Myths and Legends of the North American Indians*. London: George C. Harrap, 1914. A collection of tales and legends of the earliest North American peoples, along with early opinions on origins, beliefs, and superstitions of Native Americans.

Karl Taube, *Aztec and Maya Myths*. London and Austin: British Museum Press and University of Texas Press, 1993. A comprehensive text containing a detailed exploration of Aztec and Mayan cultures along with explanations of their most important myths.

Angela P. Thomas, *Egyptian Gods and Myths*. Buckinghamshire, England: Shire Publications, 1986. A strong, easy-to-read overview of all the major deities and myths of ancient Egypt.

Internet Sources

Lady Gregory, *Cuchulain of Muirthemne*. www.belinus.co.uk/folklore/FaerypiecesGregory2.htm. December 20, 2000. An online resource that posts in full the 1902 collection of the Ulster Cycle of Irish-Celtic mythology as translated and compiled by turn-of-the-century Irish literary figure Lady Gregory. The final section, Chapter XX, includes the events surrounding the Irish hero Cuchulain's final battle as well as the circumstances of his death.

The Voyage of Bran, www.as.wvu.edu/eng101/www/clc/vob/bran.html. *The Voyage of Bran*, an anonymous medieval Irish saga, was translated into English from the Old Irish by Kuno Meyer in 1890. This work is now accessible to all via the World Wide Web by the Eberly College of Arts and Sciences at West Virginia University.

Index

Picture Credits

About the Author

Michael J. Wyly received his Master of Fine Arts in creative writing from California State University, Long Beach. He is an instructor of English literature and language at California State University, Long Beach. He has also functioned as a fiction and poetry editor for several small-press publications. Wyly is currently on leave from his teaching duties and lives and writes in France.